DOVER · THRIFT · EDITIONS

Rhetoric

ARISTOTLE

Translated by
W. Rhys Roberts

DOVER PUBLICATIONS, INC.
Mineola, New York

DOVER THRIFT EDITIONS

GENERAL EDITOR: PAUL NEGRI
EDITOR OF THIS VOLUME: JENNY BAK

Bibliographical Note

This Dover edition, first published in 2004, is an unabridged republication of *Rhetoric* from volume nine of *The Works of Aristotle*, translated into English under the editorship of W. D. Ross, and originally published by Oxford University Press, London, from 1910–1931. The introductory Note has been specially prepared for this edition. The numbers located on the outer margins of the text refer to the page and line placement of the Bekker edition of this work. Due to the shifting of the text, the numbers in this edition are approximations of the original Bekker index.

Library of Congress Cataloging-in-Publication Data

Aristotle.
   [Rhetoric. English]
   Rhetoric / Aristotle ; translated by W. Rhys Roberts. — Dover thrift eds.
      p. cm.
   "Unabridged republication of Rhetoric from volume nine of The works of Aristotle, originally published by Oxford University Press, London, in 1924"—Copyright p.
   Includes index.
   ISBN-13: 978-0-486-43793-4
   ISBN-10: 0-486-43793-0
   1. Rhetoric—Early works to 1800. 2. Poetry—Early works to 1800. 3. Aesthetics—Early works to 1800. I. Roberts, W. Rhys (William Rhys), 1858–1929. II. Title.

PN173.A7R6 2004
808'.00938—dc22

                                    2004052176

Manufactured in the United States by Courier Corporation
43793007   2014
www.doverpublications.com

Note

MORE THAN two millennia after his death, Aristotle remains one of the foremost philosophers in history. His creation of the Aristotelian system of logic, as well as his unprecedented forays into science, politics, and metaphysics, advanced Western intellectual thought from ancient times to as far as the seventeenth century.

Aristotle was born in 384 B.C. in the town of Stagira on the Macedonian peninsula in northern Greece. His father, a court physician, died during Aristotle's childhood, and the youth was subsequently sent to study under Plato at the Academy in Athens. He would remain under Plato's tutelage for twenty years, until 348 B.C. He developed a shining reputation as a student, especially in the field of rhetoric. With the death of his mentor, Aristotle left the Academy and traveled to Assus, where he helped establish a school to further expand Greek interests into Asia Minor. In 342 B.C., by then a well-known scholar, Aristotle was summoned to Pella by Philip II of Macedon to tutor his son, who would later be known as Alexander the Great.

After a lengthy absence from Athens, Aristotle returned in 335 B.C. to found a school to rival his alma mater. Named the Lyceum due to its proximity to the temple of Apollo Lyceius, the school focused on the fields of biology and history, as well as philosophy and other branches of science. Twelve years later, Aristotle retired to the island of Eubœa, his mother's homeland, where he died from a stomach ailment in 322 B.C.

In *Rhetoric*, possibly the first work to be written on the subject, Aristotle defines rhetoric as the study of the means of persuasion. His validation of rhetoric as a legitimate skill was a significant divergence from Plato's belief that it is a practice of flattery and artifice, with little relationship to truth. Aristotle impresses the importance of the audience (or "judge") when presenting an argument, and describes the different forms of rhetoric, providing examples and advice for each. Likely derived from his lecture notes from the Academy and the Lyceum, this influential work remains the definitive analysis of rhetoric and its role in Western intellectual theory.

Contents

subjects, and the premises from which it argues, are in the main
such as present alternative possibilities in the sphere of human action; and it must adapt itself to an audience of untrained thinkers
who cannot follow a long train of reasoning. The premises from
which enthymemes are formed are 'probabilities' and 'signs'; and
signs are either fallible or infallible, in which latter case they are
termed τεκμήρια. The lines of argument, or topics, which enthymemes follow may be distinguished as common (or, general)
and special (i.e. special to a single study, such as natural science
or ethics). The special lines should be used discreetly, if the
rhetorician is not to find himself deserting his own field for
another.

persons affected may be (*a*) the entire community, (*b*) individual
members of it. A wrongdoer must either understand and intend
the action, or not understand and intend it. In the former case, he
must be acting either from deliberate choice or from passion. It is
deliberate purpose that constitutes wickedness and criminal guilt.
Unwritten law (1) includes in its purview the conduct that springs
from exceptional goodness or badness, e.g. our behaviour towards
benefactors and friends; (2) makes up for the defects in a community's written code of law. This second kind is equity. Its existence partly is, and partly is not, intended by legislators; not
intended, where they have noticed no defect in the law; intended,
where they find themselves unable to define things exactly, and
are obliged to legislate as if that held good always which in fact
only holds good usually. — Further remarks on the nature and
scope of equity.

BOOK II

exists to affect the giving of decisions, the orator must not only try to make the argument of his speech demonstrative and worthy of belief; he must also (1) make his own character look right and (2) put his hearers, who are to decide, into the right frame of mind. As to his own character: he should make his audience feel that he possesses prudence, virtue, and goodwill. This is especially important in a deliberative assembly. In the law courts it is especially important that he should be able to influence the emotions, or moral affections, of the jury who try the case. Definition of the several emotions. In regard to each emotion we must consider (*a*) the states of mind in which it is felt; (*b*) the people towards whom it is felt; (*c*) the grounds on which it is felt.

this advantage, that they are comparatively easy to invent, whereas it is hard to find parallels among actual past events.

putting forward a statement contrary to it; (δ) by quoting previous decisions.

Chapter 26   115

Correction of two errors, possible or actual: (1) Amplification and Depreciation do not constitute an element of enthymeme, in the sense of 'a line of enthymematic argument'; (2) refutative enthymemes are not a different species from constructive. This brings to an end the treatment of the thought-element of rhetoric—the way to invent and refute persuasive arguments. There remain the subjects of (A) style and (B) arrangement.

Book III

Chapter 1   119

(A) Style. It is not enough to know what to say; we must also say it in the right way. Upon the subject of delivery (which presents itself here) no systematic treatise has been composed, though this art has much to do with oratory (as with poetry). The matter has, however, been touched upon by Thrasymachus in his 'Appeals to Pity.' As to the place of style: the right thing in speaking really is that we should fight our case with no help beyond the bare facts; and yet the arts of language cannot help having a small but real importance, whatever it is we have to expound to others. Through the influence of the poets, the language of oratorical prose at first took a poetical colour, as in the case of Gorgias. But the language of prose is distinct from that of poetry; and, further, the writers of tragic poetry itself have now given up those words, not used in ordinary talk, which adorned the early drama.

Chapter 2   121

Still, in the main, the same definition and methods apply alike to poetical and to prose style. Style, to be good, must be clear; it must also be appropriate, avoiding both meanness and excess of dignity. How these qualities may be attained. Rare, compound, and invented words must be used sparingly in prose; in which, over and above the regular and proper terms for things, metaphorical terms only can be used with advantage, and even these need care. The language of oratorical prose should, in fact, be like that of ordinary conversation. Some discussion of metaphor.

reasoner.' Hints as to the order in which arguments should be presented. As to character: you cannot well say complimentary things about yourself or abusive things about another, but you can put such remarks into the mouth of some third person.

Interrogation and Jests. The best moment to employ interrogation is when your opponent has so answered one question that the putting of just one more lands him in absurdity. In replying to questions, you must meet them, if they are ambiguous, by drawing reasonable distinctions, not by a curt answer. — Jests are supposed to be of some service in controversy. Gorgias said that you should kill your opponents' earnestness with jesting and their jesting with earnestness; in which he was right. Jests have been classified in the *Poetics*. 'Some are becoming to a gentleman, others are not; see that you choose such as become *you*. Irony better befits a gentleman than buffoonery; the ironical man jokes to amuse himself, the buffoon to amuse other people.'

Epilogue (Peroration, Conclusion). This has four parts. You must (1) make the audience well disposed towards yourself and ill disposed towards your opponent, (2) magnify or minimize the leading facts, (3) excite the required kind of emotion in your hearers, and (4) refresh their memories by means of a recapitulation. — In your closing words you may dispense with conjunctions, and thereby mark the difference between the oration and the peroration: 'I have done. You have heard me. The facts are before you. I ask for your judgement.'

Rhetoric

BOOK I

Chapter 1

RHETORIC is the counterpart of Dialectic. Both alike are con- 1354ª
cerned with such things as come, more or less, within the general
ken of all men and belong to no definite science. Accordingly all
men make use, more or less, of both; for to a certain extent all men
attempt to discuss statements and to maintain them, to defend 5
themselves and to attack others. Ordinary people do this either at
random or through practice and from acquired habit. Both ways
being possible, the subject can plainly be handled systematically,
for it is possible to inquire the reason why some speakers succeed
through practice and others spontaneously; and every one will at 10
once agree that such an inquiry is the function of an art.

Now, the framers of the current treatises on rhetoric have con-
structed but a small portion of that art. The modes of persuasion
are the only true constituents of the art: everything else is merely
accessory. These writers, however, say nothing about enthymemes, which are the substance of rhetorical persuasion, but 15
deal mainly with non-essentials. The arousing of prejudice, pity,
anger, and similar emotions has nothing to do with the essential
facts, but is merely a personal appeal to the man who is judging
the case. Consequently if the rules for trials which are now laid
down in some states—especially in well-governed states—were ap- 20
plied everywhere, such people would have nothing to say. All
men, no doubt, *think* that the laws should prescribe such rules,
but some, as in the court of Areopagus, give practical effect to
their thoughts and forbid talk about non-essentials. This is sound
law and custom. It is not right to pervert the judge by moving him
to anger or envy or pity—one might as well warp a carpenter's rule 25
before using it. Again, a litigant has clearly nothing to do but to
show that the alleged fact is so or is not so, that it has or has not
happened. As to whether a thing is important or unimportant, just
or unjust, the judge must surely refuse to take his instructions
from the litigants: he must decide for himself all such points as the 30
law-giver has not already defined for him.

3

Now, it is of great moment that well-drawn laws should themselves define all the points they possibly can and leave as few as may be to the decision of the judges; and this for several reasons. 1354ᵇ First, to find one man, or a few men, who are sensible persons and capable of legislating and administering justice is easier than to find a large number. Next, laws are made after long consideration, whereas decisions in the courts are given at short notice, which makes it hard for those who try the case to satisfy the claims of justice and expediency. The weightiest reason of all is that the decision of the lawgiver is not particular but prospective and general, whereas members of the assembly and the jury find it *their* duty to decide on definite cases brought before them. They will often have allowed themselves to be so much influenced by feelings of friendship or hatred or self-interest that they lose any clear vision of the truth and have their judgement obscured by considerations of personal pleasure or pain. In general, then, the judge should, we say, be allowed to decide as few things as possible. But questions as to whether something has happened or has not happened, will be or will not be, is or is not, must of necessity be left to the judge, since the lawgiver cannot foresee them. If this is so, it is evident that any one who lays down rules about other matters, such as what must be the contents of the 'introduction' or the 'narration' or any of the other divisions of a speech, is theorizing about non-essentials as if they belonged to the art. The only question with which these writers here deal is how to put the judge into a given frame of mind. About the orator's proper modes of persuasion they have nothing to tell us; nothing, that is, about how to gain skill in enthymemes.

Hence it comes that, although the same systematic principles apply to political as to forensic oratory, and although the former is a nobler business, and fitter for a citizen, than that which concerns the relations of private individuals, these authors say nothing about political oratory, but try, one and all, to write treatises on the way to plead in court. The reason for this is that in political oratory there is less inducement to talk about non-essentials. Political oratory is less given to unscrupulous practices than forensic, because it treats of wider issues. In a political debate the man who is forming a judgement is making a decision about his own vital interests. There is no need, therefore, to prove anything except that the facts are what the supporter of a measure maintains they are. In forensic oratory this is not enough; to conciliate the listener is what pays here. It is other people's affairs that are to be decided, so that the judges, intent on their own satisfaction and listening with

partiality, surrender themselves to the disputants instead of judging between them. Hence in many places, as we have said already,   1355ª
irrelevant speaking is forbidden in the law-courts: in the public assembly those who have to form a judgement are themselves well
able to guard against that.

It is clear, then, that rhetorical study, in its strict sense, is concerned with the modes of persuasion. Persuasion is clearly a sort
of demonstration, since we are most fully persuaded when we con-   5
sider a thing to have been demonstrated. The orator's demonstration is an enthymeme, and this is, in general, the most effective of
the modes of persuasion. The enthymeme is a sort of syllogism,
and the consideration of syllogisms of all kinds, without distinction, is the business of dialectic, either of dialectic as a whole or of
one of its branches. It follows plainly, therefore, that he who is best   10
able to see how and from what elements a syllogism is produced
will also be best skilled in the enthymeme, when he has further
learnt what its subject-matter is and in what respects it differs from
the syllogism of strict logic. The true and the approximately true
are apprehended by the same faculty; it may also be noted that   15
men have a sufficient natural instinct for what is true, and usually
do arrive at the truth. Hence the man who makes a good guess at
truth is likely to make a good guess at probabilities.

It has now been shown that the ordinary writers on rhetoric treat
of non-essentials; it has also been shown why they have inclined
more towards the forensic branch of oratory.   20

Rhetoric is useful (1) because things that are true and things
that are just have a natural tendency to prevail over their opposites, so that if the decisions of judges are not what they ought to
be, the defeat must be due to the speakers themselves, and they
must be blamed accordingly. Moreover, (2) before some audiences not even the possession of the exactest knowledge will make   25
it easy for what we say to produce conviction. For argument based
on knowledge implies instruction, and there are people whom
one cannot instruct. Here, then, we must use, as our modes of persuasion and argument, notions possessed by everybody, as we
observed in the *Topics* when dealing with the way to handle a popular audience. Further, (3) we must be able to employ persuasion,
just as strict reasoning can be employed, on opposite sides of a   30
question, not in order that we may in practice employ it in both
ways (for we must not make people believe what is wrong), but in
order that we may see clearly what the facts are, and that, if another man argues unfairly, we on our part may be able to confute
him. No other of the arts draws opposite conclusions: dialectic and   35

rhetoric alone do this. Both these arts draw opposite conclusions impartially. Nevertheless, the underlying facts do not lend themselves equally well to the contrary views. No; things that are true and things that are better are, by their nature, practically always easier to prove and easier to believe in. Again, (4) it is absurd to
1355b hold that a man ought to be ashamed of being unable to defend himself with his limbs, but not of being unable to defend himself with speech and reason, when the use of rational speech is more distinctive of a human being than the use of his limbs. And if it be objected that one who uses such power of speech unjustly might do great harm, *that* is a charge which may be made in common against all good things except virtue, and above all against the
5   things that are most useful, as strength, health, wealth, generalship. A man can confer the greatest of benefits by a right use of these, and inflict the greatest of injuries by using them wrongly.

It is clear, then, that rhetoric is not bound up with a single definite class of subjects, but is as universal as dialectic; it is clear, also, that it is useful. It is clear, further, that its function is not sim-
10   ply to succeed in persuading, but rather to discover the means of coming as near such success as the circumstances of each particular case allow. In this it resembles all other arts. For example, it is not the function of medicine simply to make a man quite healthy, but to put him as far as may be on the road to health; it is possible to give excellent treatment even to those who can never enjoy sound health. Furthermore, it is plain that it is the function
15   of one and the same art to discern the real and the apparent means of persuasion, just as it is the function of dialectic to discern the real and the apparent syllogism. What makes a man a 'sophist' is not his faculty, but his moral purpose. In rhetoric, however, the term 'rhetorician' may describe either the speaker's knowledge of
20   the art, or his moral purpose. In dialectic it is different: a man is a 'sophist' because he has a certain kind of moral purpose, a 'dialectician' in respect, not of his moral purpose, but of his faculty.

Let us now try to give some account of the systematic principles of Rhetoric itself—of the right method and means of succeeding in the object we set before us. We must make as it were a fresh
25   start, and before going further define what rhetoric is.

Chapter 2

Rhetoric may be defined as the faculty of observing in any given case the available means of persuasion. This is not a function of any other art. Every other art can instruct or persuade about its own particular subject-matter; for instance, medicine about what is healthy and unhealthy, geometry about the properties of magnitudes, arithmetic about numbers, and the same is true of the other arts and sciences. But rhetoric we look upon as the power of observing the means of persuasion on almost any subject presented to us; and that is why we say that, in its technical character, it is not concerned with any special or definite class of subjects. 30

Of the modes of persuasion some belong strictly to the art of rhetoric and some do not. By the latter I mean such things as are not supplied by the speaker but are there at the outset—witnesses, evidence given under torture, written contracts, and so on. By the former I mean such as we can ourselves construct by means of the principles of rhetoric. The one kind has merely to be used, the other has to be invented.

Of the modes of persuasion furnished by the spoken word there 1356ᵃ are three kinds. The first kind depends on the personal character of the speaker; the second on putting the audience into a certain frame of mind; the third on the proof, or apparent proof, provided by the words of the speech itself. Persuasion is achieved by the speaker's personal character when the speech is so spoken as to make us think him credible. We believe good men more fully and more readily than others: this is true generally whatever the question is, and absolutely true where exact certainty is impossible and opinions are divided. This kind of persuasion, like the others, should be achieved by what the speaker says, not by what people think of his character before he begins to speak. It is not true, as some writers assume in their treatises on rhetoric, that the personal goodness revealed by the speaker contributes nothing to his power of persuasion; on the contrary, his character may almost be called the most effective means of persuasion he possesses. Secondly, persuasion may come through the hearers, when the speech stirs their emotions. Our judgements when we are pleased and friendly are not the same as when we are pained and hostile. It is towards producing these effects, as we maintain, that present-day writers on rhetoric direct the whole of their efforts. This subject shall be treated in detail when we come to speak of the emotions. Thirdly, persuasion is effected through the speech itself when we have proved a truth or an apparent truth by means of the persuasive arguments suitable to the case in question.

There are, then, these three means of effecting persuasion. The man who is to be in command of them must, it is clear, be able (1) to reason logically, (2) to understand human character and

goodness in their various forms, and (3) to understand the emotions—that is, to name them and describe them, to know their
25 causes and the way in which they are excited. It thus appears that
rhetoric is an offshoot of dialectic and also of ethical studies.
Ethical studies may fairly be called political; and for this reason
rhetoric masquerades as political science, and the professors of it
as political experts—sometimes from want of education, sometimes from ostentation, sometimes owing to other human failings.
30 As a matter of fact, it is a branch of dialectic and similar to it, as
we said at the outset. Neither rhetoric nor dialectic is the scientific
study of any one separate subject: both are faculties for providing
arguments. This is perhaps a sufficient account of their scope and
35 of how they are related to each other.

With regard to the persuasion achieved by proof or apparent
1356ᵇ proof: just as in dialectic there is induction on the one hand and
syllogism or apparent syllogism on the other, so it is in rhetoric.
The example is an induction, the enthymeme is a syllogism, and
the apparent enthymeme is an apparent syllogism. I call the en-
5 thymeme a rhetorical syllogism, and the example a rhetorical induction. Every one who effects persuasion through proof does in
fact use either enthymemes or examples: there is no other way.
And since every one who proves anything at all is bound to use either syllogisms or inductions (and this is clear to us from the
Analytics), it must follow that enthymemes are syllogisms and ex-
10 amples are inductions. The difference between example and enthymeme is made plain by the passages in the *Topics* where
induction and syllogism have already been discussed. When we
base the proof of a proposition on a number of similar cases, this
is induction in dialectic, example in rhetoric; when it is shown
15 that, certain propositions being true, a further and quite distinct
proposition must also be true in consequence, whether invariably
or usually, this is called syllogism in dialectic, enthymeme in
rhetoric. It is plain also that each of these types of oratory has its
advantages. Types of oratory, I say: for what has been said in the
20 *Methodics* applies equally well here; in some oratorical styles examples prevail, in others enthymemes; and in like manner, some
orators are better at the former and some at the latter. Speeches
that rely on examples are as persuasive as the other kind, but those
which rely on enthymemes excite the louder applause. The
25 sources of examples and enthymemes, and their proper uses, we
will discuss later. Our next step is to define the processes themselves more clearly.

A statement is persuasive and credible either because it is di-

rectly self-evident or because it appears to be proved from other
statements that are so. In either case it is persuasive because there
is somebody whom it persuades. But none of the arts theorize
about individual cases. Medicine, for instance, does not theorize
about what will help to cure Socrates or Callias, but only about   30
what will help to cure any or all of a given class of patients: this
alone is business: individual cases are so infinitely various that no
systematic knowledge of them is possible. In the same way the theory of rhetoric is concerned not with what seems probable to a
given individual like Socrates or Hippias, but with what seems
probable to men of a given type; and this is true of dialectic also.   35
Dialectic does not construct its syllogisms out of any haphazard
materials, such as the fancies of crazy people, but out of materials
that call for discussion; and rhetoric, too, draws upon the regular
subjects of debate. The duty of rhetoric is to deal with such mat-   1357ᵃ
ters as we deliberate upon without arts or systems to guide us, in
the hearing of persons who cannot take in at a glance a complicated argument, or follow a long chain of reasoning. The subjects
of our deliberation are such as seem to present us with alternative   5
possibilities: about things that could not have been, and cannot
now or in the future be, other than they are, nobody who takes
them to be of this nature wastes his time in deliberation.

It is possible to form syllogisms and draw conclusions from the
results of previous syllogisms; or, on the other hand, from premisses which have not been thus proved, and at the same time are   10
so little accepted that they call for proof. Reasonings of the former
kind will necessarily be hard to follow owing to their length, for we
assume an audience of untrained thinkers; those of the latter kind
will fail to win assent, because they are based on premisses that are
not generally admitted or believed.

The enthymeme and the example must, then, deal with what is
in the main contingent, the example being an induction, and the   15
enthymeme a syllogism, about such matters. The enthymeme
must consist of few propositions, fewer often than those which
make up the normal syllogism. For if any of these propositions is
a familiar fact, there is no need even to mention it; the hearer adds
it himself. Thus, to show that Dorieus has been victor in a contest
for which the prize is a crown, it is enough to say 'For he has been   20
victor in the Olympic games', without adding 'And in the
Olympic games the prize is a crown', a fact which everybody
knows.

There are few facts of the 'necessary' type that can form the
basis of rhetorical syllogisms. Most of the things about which we

25 make decisions, and into which therefore we inquire, present us with alternative possibilities. For it is about our actions that we deliberate and inquire, and all our actions have a contingent character; hardly any of them are determined by necessity. Again, conclusions that state what is merely usual or possible must be drawn from premises that do the same, just as 'necessary' conclusions must be drawn from 'necessary' premises; this too is clear to us

30 from the *Analytics*. It is evident, therefore, that the propositions forming the basis of enthymemes, though some of them may be 'necessary', will most of them be only usually true. Now the materials of enthymemes are Probabilities and Signs, which we can see must correspond respectively with the propositions that are generally and those that are necessarily true. A Probability is a

35 thing that usually happens; not, however, as some definitions would suggest, anything whatever that usually happens, but only if it belongs to the class of the 'contingent' or 'variable'. It bears the same relation to that in respect of which it is probable as the uni-

1357ᵇ versal bears to the particular. Of Signs, one kind bears the same relation to the statement it supports as the particular bears to the universal, the other the same as the universal bears to the particular. The infallible kind is a 'complete proof' (τεκμήριον); the fallible kind has no specific name. By infallible signs I mean those

5 on which syllogisms proper may be based: and this shows us why this kind of Sign is called 'complete proof': when people think that what they have said cannot be refuted, they then think that they are bringing forward a 'complete proof', meaning that the matter has now been demonstrated and completed (πεπερασμένον); for the word πέρας has the same meaning (of

10 'end' or 'boundary') as the word τέκμαρ in the ancient tongue. Now the one kind of Sign (that which bears to the proposition it supports the relation of particular to universal) may be illustrated thus. Suppose it were said, 'The fact that Socrates was wise and just is a sign that the wise are just'. Here we certainly have a Sign; but even though the proposition be true, the argument is refutable, since it does not form a syllogism. Suppose, on the other

15 hand, it were said, 'The fact that he has a fever is a sign that he is ill', or, 'The fact that she is giving milk is a sign that she has lately borne a child'. Here we have the infallible kind of Sign, the only kind that constitutes a complete proof, since it is the only kind that, if the particular statement is true, is irrefutable. The other kind of Sign, that which bears to the proposition it supports the relation of universal to particular, might be illustrated by saying, 'The fact that he breathes fast is a sign that he has a fever'. This ar-

gument also is refutable, even if the statement about the fast   20
breathing be true, since a man may breathe hard without having
a fever.

It has, then, been stated above what is the nature of a
Probability, of a Sign, and of a complete proof, and what are the
differences between them. In the *Analytics* a more explicit description has been given of these points; it is there shown why
some of these reasonings can be put into syllogisms and some
cannot.

The 'example' has already been described as one kind of in-   25
duction; and the special nature of the subject-matter that distin-
guishes it from the other kinds has also been stated above. Its
relation to the proposition it supports is not that of part to whole,
nor whole to part, nor whole to whole, but of part to part, or like
to like. When two statements are of the same order, but one is
more familiar than the other, the former is an 'example'. The ar-   30
gument may, for instance, be that Dionysius, in asking as he does
for a bodyguard, is scheming to make himself a despot. For in the
past Peisistratus kept asking for a bodyguard in order to carry out
such a scheme, and did make himself a despot as soon as he got
it; and so did Theagenes at Megara; and in the same way all other
instances known to the speaker are made into examples, in order
to show what is not yet known, that Dionysius has the same pur-   35
pose in making the same request: all these being instances of the
one general principle, that a man who asks for a bodyguard is
scheming to make himself a despot. We have now described the   1358ª
sources of those means of persuasion which are popularly supposed to be demonstrative.

There is an important distinction between two sorts of enthymemes that has been wholly overlooked by almost everybody—one that also subsists between the syllogisms treated of in
dialectic. One sort of enthymeme really belongs to rhetoric, as one
sort of syllogism really belongs to dialectic; but the other sort re-   5
ally belongs to other arts and faculties, whether to those we already
exercise or to those we have not yet acquired. Missing this distinction, people fail to notice that the more correctly they handle their
particular subject the further they are getting away from pure
rhetoric or dialectic. This statement will be clearer if expressed
more fully. I mean that the proper subjects of dialectical and   10
rhetorical syllogisms are the things with which we say the regular
or universal Lines of Argument are concerned, that is to say those
lines of argument that apply equally to questions of right conduct,
natural science, politics, and many other things that have nothing

to do with one another. Take, for instance, the line of argument concerned with 'the more or less'. On this line of argument it is
15 equally easy to base a syllogism or enthymeme about any of what nevertheless are essentially disconnected subjects—right conduct, natural science, or anything else whatever. But there are also those special Lines of Argument which are based on such propositions as apply only to particular groups or classes of things. Thus there are propositions about natural science on which it is impossible to base any enthymeme or syllogism about ethics, and other propo-
20 sitions about ethics on which nothing can be based about natural science. The same principle applies throughout. The general Lines of Argument have no special subject-matter, and therefore will not increase our understanding of any particular class of things. On the other hand, the better the selection one makes of propositions suitable for special Lines of Argument, the nearer one comes, unconsciously, to setting up a science that is distinct
25 from dialectic and rhetoric. One may succeed in stating the required principles, but one's science will be no longer dialectic or rhetoric, but the science to which the principles thus discovered belong. Most enthymemes are in fact based upon these particular or special Lines of Argument; comparatively few on the common or general kind. As in the *Topics*, therefore, so in this work, we
30 must distinguish, in dealing with enthymemes, the special and the general Lines of Argument on which they are to be founded. By special Lines of Argument I mean the propositions peculiar to each several class of things, by general those common to all classes alike. We may begin with the special Lines of Argument. But, first of all, let us classify rhetoric into its varieties. Having distinguished these we may deal with them one by one, and try to discover the
35 elements of which each is composed, and the propositions each must employ.

Chapter 3

Rhetoric falls into three divisions, determined by the three classes of listeners to speeches. For of the three elements in speech-making—speaker, subject, and person addressed—it is the last
1358ᵇ one, the hearer, that determines the speech's end and object. The hearer must be either a judge, with a decision to make about things past or future, or an observer. A member of the assembly de-
5 cides about future events, a juryman about past events: while those who merely decide on the orator's skill are observers. From this it

follows that there are three divisions of oratory—(1) political, (2) forensic, and (3) the ceremonial oratory of display.

Political speaking urges us either to do or not to do something: one of these two courses is always taken by private counsellors, as well as by men who address public assemblies. Forensic speaking either attacks or defends somebody: one or other of these two things must always be done by the parties in a case. The ceremonial oratory of display either praises or censures somebody. These three kinds of rhetoric refer to three different kinds of time. The political orator is concerned with the future: it is about things to be done hereafter that he advises, for or against. The party in a case at law is concerned with the past; one man accuses the other, and the other defends himself, with reference to things already done. The ceremonial orator is, properly speaking, concerned with the present, since all men praise or blame in view of the state of things existing at the time, though they often find it useful also to recall the past and to make guesses at the future.

Rhetoric has three distinct ends in view, one for each of its three kinds. The political orator aims at establishing the expediency or the harmfulness of a proposed course of action; if he urges its acceptance, he does so on the ground that it will do good; if he urges its rejection, he does so on the ground that it will do harm; and all other points, such as whether the proposal is just or unjust, honourable or dishonourable, he brings in as subsidiary and relative to this main consideration. Parties in a law-case aim at establishing the justice or injustice of some action, and they too bring in all other points as subsidiary and relative to this one. Those who praise or attack a man aim at proving him worthy of honour or the reverse, and they too treat all other considerations with reference to this one.

That the three kinds of rhetoric do aim respectively at the three ends we have mentioned is shown by the fact that speakers will sometimes not try to establish anything else. Thus, the litigant will sometimes not deny that a thing has happened or that he has done harm. But that he is guilty of injustice he will never admit; otherwise there would be no need of a trial. So too, political orators often make any concession short of admitting that they are recommending their hearers to take an inexpedient course or not to take an expedient one. The question whether it is not *unjust* for a city to enslave its innocent neighbours often does not trouble them at all. In like manner those who praise or censure a man do not consider whether his acts have been expedient or not, but often make it a ground of actual praise that he has neglected his

10

15

20

25

30

35

1359ᵃ

own interest to do what was honourable. Thus, they praise Achilles because he championed his fallen friend Patroclus, though he knew that this meant death, and that otherwise he need not die: yet while to die thus was the nobler thing for him to do, 5 the expedient thing was to live on.

It is evident from what has been said that it is these three subjects, more than any others, about which the orator must be able to have propositions at his command. Now the propositions of Rhetoric are Complete Proofs, Probabilities, and Signs. Every 10 kind of syllogism is composed of propositions, and the enthymeme is a particular kind of syllogism composed of the aforesaid propositions.

Since only possible actions, and not impossible ones, can ever have been done in the past or the present, and since things which have not occurred, or will not occur, also cannot have been done 15 or be going to be done, it is necessary for the political, the forensic, and the ceremonial speaker alike to be able to have at their command propositions about the possible and the impossible, and about whether a thing has or has not occurred, will or will not occur. Further, all men, in giving praise or blame, in urging us to accept or reject proposals for action, in accusing others or defending themselves, attempt not only to prove the points mentioned 20 tioned but also to show that the good or the harm, the honour or disgrace, the justice or injustice, is great or small, either absolutely or relatively; and therefore it is plain that we must also have at our command propositions about greatness or smallness and the greater or the lesser—propositions both universal and particular. Thus, we must be able to say which is the greater or lesser good, 25 the greater or lesser act of justice or injustice; and so on.

Such, then, are the subjects regarding which we are inevitably bound to master the propositions relevant to them. We must now discuss each particular class of these subjects in turn, namely those dealt with in political, in ceremonial, and lastly in legal, oratory.

Chapter 4

30 First, then, we must ascertain what are the kinds of things, good or bad, about which the political orator offers counsel. For he does not deal with all things, but only with such as may or may not take place. Concerning things which exist or will exist inevitably, or which cannot possibly exist or take place, no counsel can be

given. Nor, again, can counsel be given about the whole class of
things which may or may not take place; for this class includes
some good things that occur naturally, and some that occur by ac-   35
cident; and about these it is useless to offer counsel. Clearly counsel can only be given on matters about which people deliberate;
matters, namely, that ultimately depend on ourselves, and which
we have it in our power to set going. For we turn a thing over in
our mind until we have reached the point of seeing whether we   1359^b
can do it or not.

Now to enumerate and classify accurately the usual subjects of
public business, and further to frame, as far as possible, true definitions of them, is a task which we must not attempt on the present
occasion. For it does not belong to the art of rhetoric, but to a more   5
instructive art and a more real branch of knowledge; and as it is,
rhetoric has been given a far wider subject-matter than strictly belongs to it. The truth is, as indeed we have said already, that
rhetoric is a combination of the science of logic and of the ethical   10
branch of politics; and it is partly like dialectic, partly like sophisti-
cal reasoning. But the more we try to make either dialectic or
rhetoric not, what they really are, practical faculties, but sciences,
the more we shall inadvertently be destroying their true nature; for   15
we shall be re-fashioning them and shall be passing into the region
of sciences dealing with definite subjects rather than simply with
words and forms of reasoning. Even here, however, we will mention those points which it is of practical importance to distinguish,
their fuller treatment falling naturally to political science.

The main matters on which all men deliberate and on which
political speakers make speeches are some five in number: ways   20
and means, war and peace, national defence, imports and exports,
and legislation.

As to Ways and Means, then, the intending speaker will need to
know the number and extent of the country's sources of revenue,
so that, if any is being overlooked, it may be added, and, if any is   25
defective, it may be increased. Further, he should know all the expenditure of the country, in order that, if any part of it is superfluous, it may be abolished, or, if any is too large, it may be reduced.
For men become richer not only by increasing their existing
wealth but also by reducing their expenditure. A comprehensive
view of these questions cannot be gained solely from experience   30
in home affairs; in order to advise on such matters a man must be
keenly interested in the methods worked out in other lands.

As to Peace and War, he must know the extent of the military
strength of his country, both actual and potential, and also the

35 nature of that actual and potential strength; and further, what wars
his country has waged, and how it has waged them. He must know
these facts not only about his own country, but also about neighbouring countries; and also about countries with which war is
likely, in order that peace may be maintained with those stronger
than his own, and that his own may have power to make war or not
1360ᵃ against those that are weaker. He should know, too, whether the
military power of another country is like or unlike that of his own;
for this is a matter that may affect their relative strength. With the
same end in view he must, besides, have studied the wars of other
countries as well as those of his own, and the way they ended; sim-
5   ilar causes are likely to have similar results.

With regard to National Defence: he ought to know all about
the methods of defence in actual use, such as the strength and
character of the defensive force and the positions of the forts—this
last means that he must be well acquainted with the lie of the
10 country—in order that a garrison may be increased if it is too
small or removed if it is not wanted, and that the strategic points
may be guarded with special care.

With regard to the Food Supply: he must know what outlay will
meet the needs of his country; what kinds of food are produced at
home and what imported; and what articles must be exported or
imported. This last he must know in order that agreements and
15 commercial treaties may be made with the countries concerned.
There are, indeed, two sorts of state to which he must see that his
countrymen give no cause for offence, states stronger than his
own, and states with which it is advantageous to trade.

But while he must, for security's sake, be able to take all this
into account, he must before all things understand the subject of
legislation; for it is on a country's laws that its whole welfare
20 depends. He must, therefore, know how many different forms of
constitution there are; under what conditions each of these will
prosper and by what internal developments or external attacks
each of them tends to be destroyed. When I speak of destruction
through internal developments I refer to the fact that all constitutions, except the best one of all, are destroyed both by not being
pushed far enough and by being pushed too far. Thus, democracy
25 loses its vigour, and finally passes into oligarchy, not only when it
is not pushed far enough, but also when it is pushed a great deal
too far; just as the aquiline and the snub nose not only turn into
normal noses by not being aquiline or snub enough, but also by
being too violently aquiline or snub arrive at a condition in which
they no longer look like noses at all.

It is useful, in framing laws, not only to study the past history of one's own country, in order to understand which constitution is desirable for it now, but also to have a knowledge of the constitutions of other nations, and so to learn for what kinds of nation the various kinds of constitution are suited. From this we can see that books of travel are useful aids to legislation, since from these we may learn the laws and customs of different races. The political speaker will also find the researches of historians useful. But all this is the business of political science and not of rhetoric.

These, then, are the most important kinds of information which the political speaker must possess. Let us now go back and state the premisses from which he will have to argue in favour of adopting or rejecting measures regarding these and other matters.

30

35

1360ᵇ

Chapter 5

It may be said that every individual man and all men in common aim at a certain end which determines what they choose and what they avoid. This end, to sum it up briefly, is happiness and its constituents. Let us, then, by way of illustration only, ascertain what is in general the nature of happiness, and what are the elements of its constituent parts. For all advice to do things or not to do them is concerned with happiness and with the things that make for or against it; whatever creates or increases happiness or some part of happiness, we ought to do; whatever destroys or hampers happiness, or gives rise to its opposite, we ought not to do.

5

10

We may define happiness as prosperity combined with virtue; or as independence of life; or as the secure enjoyment of the maximum of pleasure; or as a good condition of property and body, together with the power of guarding one's property and body and making use of them. That happiness is one or more of these things, pretty well everybody agrees.

15

From this definition of happiness it follows that its constituent parts are:—good birth, plenty of friends, good friends, wealth, good children, plenty of children, a happy old age, also such bodily excellences as health, beauty, strength, large stature, athletic powers, together with fame, honour, good luck, and virtue. A man cannot fail to be completely independent if he possesses these internal and these external goods; for besides these there are no others to have. (Goods of the soul and of the body are internal. Good birth, friends, money, and honour are external.) Further, we think that he should possess resources and luck, in order to make his life

20

25

really secure. As we have already ascertained what happiness in
30   general is, so now let us try to ascertain what of these parts of it is.

Now good birth in a race or a state means that its members are
indigenous or ancient; that its earliest leaders were distinguished
men, and that from them have sprung many who were distinguished for qualities that we admire.

The good birth of an individual, which may come either from
the male or the female side, implies that both parents are free cit-
35   izens, and that, as in the case of the state, the founders of the line
have been notable for virtue or wealth or something else which is
highly prized, and that many distinguished persons belong to the
family, men and women, young and old.

The phrases 'possession of good children' and 'of many children' bear a quite clear meaning. Applied to a community, they
1361ᵃ   mean that its young men are numerous and of good quality: good
in regard to bodily excellences, such as stature, beauty, strength,
athletic powers; and also in regard to the excellences of the soul,
which in a young man are temperance and courage. Applied to an
5   individual, they mean that his own children are numerous and
have the good qualities we have described. Both male and female
are here included; the excellences of the latter are, in body, beauty
and stature; in soul, self-command and an industry that is not sordid. Communities as well as individuals should lack none of these
10   perfections, in their women as well as in their men. Where, as
among the Lacedaemonians, the state of women is bad, almost
half of human life is spoilt.

The constituents of wealth are: plenty of coined money and territory; the ownership of numerous, large, and beautiful estates;
also the ownership of numerous and beautiful implements, live
15   stock, and slaves. All these kinds of property are our own, are secure, gentlemanly, and useful. The useful kinds are those that are
productive, the gentlemanly kinds are those that provide enjoyment. By 'productive' I mean those from which we get our in-
come; by 'enjoyable', those from which we get nothing worth
mentioning except the use of them. The criterion of 'security' is
the ownership of property in such places and under such condi-
20   tions that the use of it is in our power; and it is 'our own' if it is in
our own power to dispose of it or keep it. By 'disposing of it' I mean
giving it away or selling it. Wealth as a whole consists in using
things rather than in owning them; it is really the activity—that is,
the use—of property that constitutes wealth.

25   Fame means being respected by everybody, or having some quality
that is desired by all men, or by most, or by the good, or by the wise.

Honour is the token of a man's being famous for doing good. It
is chiefly and most properly paid to those who have already done
good; but also to the man who can do good in future. Doing good
refers either to the preservation of life and the means of life, or to   30
wealth, or to some other of the good things which it is hard to get
either always or at that particular place or time—for many gain
honour for things which seem small, but the place and the occasion account for it. The constituents of honour are: sacrifices;
commemoration, in verse or prose; privileges; grants of land; front   35
seats at civic celebrations; state burial; statues; public maintenance; among foreigners, obeisances and giving place; and such
presents as are among various bodies of men regarded as marks of
honour. For a present is not only the bestowal of a piece of property, but also a token of honour; which explains why honour-
loving as well as money-loving persons desire it. The present
brings to both what they want; it is a piece of property, which is   1361ᵇ
what the lovers of money desire; and it brings honour, which is
what the lovers of honour desire.

The excellence of the body is health; that is, a condition
which allows us, while keeping free from disease, to have the use
of our bodies; for many people are 'healthy' as we are told   5
Herodicus was; and these no one can congratulate on their
'health', for they have to abstain from everything or nearly everything that men do.—Beauty varies with the time of life. In a
young man beauty is the possession of a body fit to endure the
exertion of running and of contests of strength; which means
that he is pleasant to look at; and therefore all-round athletes are
the most beautiful, being naturally adapted both for contests of   10
strength and for speed also. For a man in his prime, beauty is fitness for the exertion of warfare, together with a pleasant but at
the same time formidable appearance. For an old man, it is to be
strong enough for such exertion as is necessary, and to be free
from all those deformities of old age which cause pain to others.
Strength is the power of moving some one else at will; to do this,   15
you must either pull, push, lift, pin, or grip him; thus you must
be strong in all of those ways or at least in some. Excellence in
size is to surpass ordinary people in height, thickness, and
breadth by just as much as will not make one's movements   20
slower in consequence. Athletic excellence of the body consists
in size, strength, and swiftness; swiftness implying strength. He
who can fling forward his legs in a certain way, and move them
fast and far, is good at running; he who can grip and hold down
is good at wrestling; he who can drive an adversary from his   25

ground with the right blow is a good boxer: he who can do both
the last is a good pancratiast, while he who can do all is an 'all-
round' athlete.

Happiness in old age is the coming of old age slowly and pain-
lessly; for a man has not this happiness if he grows old either
quickly, or tardily but painfully. It arises both from the excellences
of the body and from good luck. If a man is not free from disease,
30   or if he is not strong, he will not be free from suffering; nor can he
continue to live a long and painless life unless he has good luck.
There is, indeed, a capacity for long life that is quite independent
of health or strength; for many people live long who lack the excellences of the body; but for our present purpose there is no use
in going into the details of this.

35   The terms 'possession of many friends' and 'possession of good
friends' need no explanation; for we define a 'friend' as one who
will always try, for your sake, to do what he takes to be good for
you. The man towards whom many feel thus has many friends; if
these are worthy men, he has good friends.

'Good luck' means the acquisition or possession of all or most,
or the most important, of those good things which are due to luck.
1362ᵃ Some of the things that are due to luck may also be due to artificial contrivance; but many are independent of art, as for example
those which are due to nature—though, to be sure, things due to
luck may actually be contrary to nature. Thus health may be due
to artificial contrivance, but beauty and stature are due to nature.
5   All such good things as excite envy are, as a class, the outcome of
good luck. Luck is also the cause of good things that happen contrary to reasonable expectation: as when, for instance, all your
brothers are ugly, but you are handsome yourself; or when you
find a treasure that everybody else has overlooked; or when a mis-
sile hits the next man and misses you; or when you are the only
10   man not to go to a place you have gone to regularly, while the others go there for the first time and are killed. All such things are
reckoned pieces of good luck.

As to virtue, it is most closely connected with the subject of
Eulogy, and therefore we will wait to define it until we come to
discuss that subject.

Chapter 6

15   It is now plain what our aims, future or actual, should be in urging, and what in deprecating, a proposal; the latter being the op-

posite of the former. Now the political or deliberative orator's aim
is utility: deliberation seeks to determine not ends but the means
to ends, i.e. what it is most useful to do. Further, utility is a good   20
thing. We ought therefore to assure ourselves of the main facts
about Goodness and Utility in general.

We may define a good thing as that which ought to be chosen
for its own sake; or as that for the sake of which we choose something else; or as that which is sought after by all things, or by all
things that have sensation or reason, or which will be sought after
by any things that acquire reason; or as that which must be pre-   25
scribed for a given individual by reason generally, or is prescribed
for him by his individual reason, this being his individual good; or
as that whose presence brings anything into a satisfactory and self-
sufficing condition; or as self-sufficiency; or as what produces,
maintains, or entails characteristics of this kind, while preventing
and destroying their opposites. One thing may entail another in ei-   30
ther of two ways—(1) simultaneously, (2) subsequently. Thus
learning entails knowledge subsequently, health entails life simultaneously. Things are productive of other things in three senses:
first, as being healthy produces health; secondly, as food produces
health; and thirdly, as exercise does—i.e. it does so usually. All this
being settled, we now see that both the acquisition of good things
and the removal of bad things must be good; the latter entails free-   35
dom from the evil things simultaneously, while the former entails
possession of the good things subsequently. The acquisition of a
greater in place of a lesser good, or of a lesser in place of a greater
evil, is also good, for in proportion as the greater exceeds the lesser   1362ᵇ
there is acquisition of good or removal of evil. The virtues, too,
must be something good; for it is by possessing these that we are
in a good condition, and they tend to produce good works and
good actions. They must be severally named and described else-   5
where. Pleasure, again, must be a good thing, since it is the nature
of all animals to aim at it. Consequently both pleasant and beautiful things must be good things, since the former are productive
of pleasure, while of the beautiful things some are pleasant and
some desirable in and for themselves.

The following is a more detailed list of things that must be   10
good. Happiness, as being desirable in itself and sufficient by itself, and as being that for whose sake we choose many other
things. Also justice, courage, temperance, magnanimity, magnificence, and all such qualities, as being excellences of the soul.
Further, health, beauty, and the like, as being bodily excellences   15
and productive of many other good things: for instance, health is

productive both of pleasure and of life, and therefore is thought
the greatest of goods, since these two things which it causes, pleasure and life, are two of the things most highly prized by ordinary
people. Wealth, again: for it is the excellence of possession, and
also productive of many other good things. Friends and friend-
20 ship: for a friend is desirable in himself and also productive of
many other good things. So, too, honour and reputation, as being
pleasant, and productive of many other good things, and usually
accompanied by the presence of the good things that cause them
to be bestowed. The faculty of speech and action; since all such
qualities are productive of what is good. Further—good parts,
strong memory, receptiveness, quickness of intuition, and the like,
25 for all such faculties are productive of what is good. Similarly, all
the sciences and arts. And life: since, even if no other good were
the result of life, it is desirable in itself. And justice, as the cause
of good to the community.

The above are pretty well all the things admittedly good. In
dealing with things whose goodness is disputed, we may argue in
30 the following ways:—That is good of which the contrary is bad.
That is good the contrary of which is to the advantage of our enemies; for example, if it is to the particular advantage of our enemies that we should be cowards, clearly courage is of particular
value to our countrymen. And generally, the contrary of that
which our enemies desire, or of that at which they rejoice, is evi-
35 dently valuable. Hence the passage beginning:

Surely would Priam exult.

This principle usually holds good, but not always, since it may
well be that our interest is sometimes the same as that of our enemies. Hence it is said that 'evils draw men together'; that is, when
1363ª the same thing is hurtful to them both.

Further: that which is not in excess is good, and that which is
greater than it should be is bad. That also is good on which much
labour or money has been spent; the mere fact of this makes it
seem good, and such a good is assumed to be an end—an end
5 reached through a long chain of means; and any end is a good.
Hence the lines beginning:

And for Priam (and Troy-town's folk) should they leave behind
them a boast;

and

Oh, it were shame
To have tarried so long and return empty-handed as erst we came;

and there is also the proverb about 'breaking the pitcher at the door'.

That which most people seek after, and which is obviously an object of contention, is also a good; for, as has been shown, that is good which is sought after by everybody, and 'most people' is taken to be equivalent to 'everybody'. That which is praised is good, since no one praises what is not good. So, again, that which is praised by our enemies [or by the worthless]; for when even those who have a grievance think a thing good, it is at once felt that every one must agree with them; our enemies can admit the fact only because it is evident, just as those must be worthless whom their friends censure and their enemies do not. (For this reason the Corinthians conceived themselves to be insulted by Simonides when he wrote:

Against the Corinthians hath Ilium no complaint.)

Again, that is good which has been distinguished by the favour of a discerning or virtuous man or woman, as Odysseus was distinguished by Athena, Helen by Theseus, Paris by the goddesses, and Achilles by Homer. And, generally speaking, all things are good which men deliberately choose to do; this will include the things already mentioned, and also whatever may be bad for their enemies or good for their friends, and at the same time practicable. Things are 'practicable' in two senses: (1) it is possible to do them, (2) it is easy to do them. Things are done 'easily' when they are done either without pain or quickly: the 'difficulty' of an act lies either in its painfulness or in the long time it takes. Again, a thing is good if it is as men wish; and they wish to have either no evil at all or at least a balance of good over evil. This last will happen where the penalty is either imperceptible or slight. Good, too, are things that are a man's very own, possessed by no one else, exceptional; for this increases the credit of having them. So are things which befit the possessors, such as whatever is appropriate to their birth or capacity, and whatever they feel they ought to have but lack—such things may indeed be trifling, but none the less men deliberately make them the goal of their action. And things easily effected; for these are practicable (in the sense of being easy); such things are those in which every one, or most people, or one's equals, or one's inferiors have succeeded. Good also are the things by which we shall gratify our friends or annoy our enemies: and the things chosen by those whom we admire: and the things for which we are fitted by nature or experience, since we think we shall succeed

more easily in these: and those in which no worthless man can
succeed, for such things bring greater praise: and those which
we do in fact desire, for what we desire is taken to be not only
pleasant but also better. Further, a man of a given disposition
1363ᵇ makes chiefly for the corresponding things: lovers of victory
make for victory, lovers of honour for honour, money-loving
men for money, and so with the rest. These, then, are the
sources from which we must derive our means of persuasion
about Good and Utility.

Chapter 7

5 Since, however, it often happens that people agree that two things
are both useful but do not agree about which is the more so, the
next step will be to treat of relative goodness and relative utility.

A thing which surpasses another may be regarded as being that
other thing plus something more, and that other thing which is
surpassed as being what is contained in the first thing. Now to call
a thing 'greater' or 'more' always implies a comparison of it with
10 one that is 'smaller' or 'less', while 'great' and 'small', 'much' and
'little', are terms used in comparison with normal magnitude. The
'great' is that which surpasses the normal, the 'small' is that which
is surpassed by the normal; and so with 'many' and 'few'.

Now we are applying the term 'good' to what is desirable for its
own sake and not for the sake of something else; to that at which
all things aim; to what they would choose if they could acquire
15 understanding and practical wisdom; and to that which tends to
produce or preserve such goods, or is always accompanied by
them. Moreover, that for the sake of which things are done is the
end (an end being that for the sake of which all else is done), and
for each individual that thing is a good which fulfils these conditions in regard to himself. It follows, then, that a greater number
of goods is a greater good than one or than a smaller number, if
that one or that smaller number is included in the count; for then
20 the larger number surpasses the smaller, and the smaller quantity
is surpassed as being contained in the larger.

Again, if the largest member of one class surpasses the largest
member of another, then the one class surpasses the other; and if
one class surpasses another, then the largest member of the one
surpasses the largest member of the other. Thus, if the tallest man
is taller than the tallest woman, then men in general are taller
25 than women. Conversely, if men in general are taller than

women, then the tallest man is taller than the tallest woman. For
the superiority of class over class is proportionate to the superiority possessed by their largest specimens. Again, where one good is
always accompanied by another, but does not always accompany
it, it is greater than the other, for the use of the second thing is   30
implied in the use of the first. A thing may be accompanied by
another in three ways, either simultaneously, subsequently, or potentially. Life accompanies health simultaneously (but not health
life), knowledge accompanies the act of learning subsequently,
cheating accompanies sacrilege potentially, since a man who has
committed sacrilege is always capable of cheating. Again, when
two things each surpass a third, that which does so by the greater
amount is the greater of the two; for it must surpass the greater as
well as the less of the other two. A thing productive of a greater
good than another is productive of is itself a greater good than   35
that other. For this conception of 'productive of a greater' has
been implied in our argument. Likewise, that which is produced
by a greater good is itself a greater good; thus, if what is wholesome is more desirable and a greater good than what gives pleasure, health too must be a greater good than pleasure. Again, a   1364ᵃ
thing which is desirable in itself is a greater good than a thing
which is not desirable in itself, as for example bodily strength
than what is wholesome, since the latter is not pursued for its own
sake, whereas the former is; and this was our definition of the
good. Again, if one of two things is an end, and the other is not,
the former is the greater good, as being chosen for its own sake
and not for the sake of something else; as, for example, exercise is
chosen for the sake of physical well-being. And of two things that   5
which stands less in need of the other, or of other things, is the
greater good, since it is more self-sufficing. (That which stands
'less' in need of others is that which needs either *fewer* or *easier*
things.) So when one thing does not exist or cannot come into existence without a second, while the second can exist without the
first, the second is the better. That which does not need something else is more self-sufficing than that which does, and presents itself as a greater good for that reason. Again, that which is a
beginning of other things is a greater good than that which is not,   10
and that which is a cause is a greater good than that which is not;
the reason being the same in each case, namely that without a
cause and a beginning nothing can exist or come into existence.
Again, where there are two sets of consequences arising from two
different beginnings or causes, the consequences of the more important beginning or cause are themselves the more important;

and conversely, that beginning or cause is itself the more impor-
15 tant which has the more important consequences. Now it is
plain, from all that has been said, that one thing may be shown
to be more important than another from two opposite points of
view: it may appear the more important (1) because it is a beginning and the other thing is not, and also (2) because it is not a beginning and the other thing is—on the ground that the end is
more important and is not a beginning. So Leodamas, when accusing Callistratus, said that the man who prompted the deed
20 was more guilty than the doer, since it would not have been done
if he had not planned it. On the other hand, when accusing
Chabrias he said that the doer was worse than the prompter, since
there would have been no deed without some one to do it; men,
said he, plot a thing only in order to carry it out.

Further, what is rare is a greater good than what is plentiful.
Thus, gold is a better thing than iron, though less useful: it is
25 harder to get, and therefore better worth getting. Reversely, it may
be argued that the plentiful is a better thing than the rare, because
we can make more use of it. For what is often useful surpasses
what is seldom useful, whence the saying

The best of things is water.

More generally: the hard thing is better than the easy, because it
is rarer: and reversely, the easy thing is better than the hard, for it
30 is as we wish it to be. That is the greater good whose contrary is
the greater evil, and whose loss affects us more. Positive goodness
and badness are more important than the mere *absence* of goodness and badness: for positive goodness and badness are ends,
which the mere absence of them cannot be. Further, in proportion as the functions of things are noble or base, the things themselves are good or bad: conversely, in proportion as the things
themselves are good or bad, their functions also are good or bad;
35 for the nature of results corresponds with that of their causes and
beginnings, and conversely the nature of causes and beginnings
corresponds with that of their results. Moreover, those things are
greater goods, superiority in which is more desirable or more honourable. Thus, keenness of sight is more desirable than keenness
1364ᵇ of smell, sight generally being more desirable than smell generally; and similarly, unusually great love of friends being more honourable than unusually great love of money, ordinary love of
friends is more honourable than ordinary love of money.
Conversely, if one of two normal things is better or nobler than the
other, an unusual degree of that thing is better or nobler than an

unusual degree of the other. Again, one thing is more honourable
or better than another if it is more honourable or better to desire
it; the importance of the object of a given instinct corresponds to
the importance of the instinct itself; and for the same reason, if
one thing is more honourable or better than another, it is more
honourable and better to desire it. Again, if one science is more
honourable and valuable than another, the activity with which it
deals is also more honourable and valuable; as is the science, so is
the reality that is its object, each science being authoritative in its
own sphere. So, also, the more valuable and honourable the object of a science, the more valuable and honourable the science itself is in consequence. Again, that which would be judged, or
which has been judged, a good thing, or a better thing than something else, by all or most people of understanding, or by the
majority of men, or by the ablest, must be so; either without qualification, or in so far as they use their understanding to form their
judgement. This is indeed a general principle, applicable to all
other judgements also; not only the goodness of things, but their
essence, magnitude, and general nature are in fact just what
knowledge and understanding will declare them to be. Here the
principle is applied to judgements of goodness, since one definition of 'good' was 'what beings that acquire understanding will
choose in any given case': from which it clearly follows that that
thing is *better* which understanding declares to be so. That, again,
is a better thing which attaches to better men, either absolutely, or
in virtue of their being better; as courage is better than strength.
And that is a greater good which would be chosen by a better man,
either absolutely, or in virtue of his being better: for instance, to
suffer wrong rather than to do wrong, for that would be the choice
of the juster man. Again, the pleasanter of two things is the better,
since *all* things pursue pleasure, and things instinctively desire
pleasurable sensation *for its own sake*; and these are two of the
characteristics by which the 'good' and the 'end' have been defined. One pleasure is greater than another if it is more unmixed
with pain, or more lasting. Again, the nobler thing is better than
the less noble, since the noble is either what is pleasant or what is
desirable in itself. And those things also are greater goods which
men desire more earnestly to bring about for themselves or for
their friends, whereas those things which they least desire to bring
about are greater evils. And those things which are more lasting
are better than those which are more fleeting, and the more secure than the less; the enjoyment of the lasting has the advantage
of being longer, and that of the secure has the advantage of suit-

ing our wishes, being there for us whenever we like. Further, in
accordance with the rule of co-ordinate terms and inflexions of
the same stem, what is true of one such related word is true of all.
35 Thus if the action qualified by the term 'brave' is more noble and
desirable than the action qualified by the term 'temperate', then
'bravery' is more desirable than 'temperance' and 'being brave'
than 'being temperate'. That, again, which is chosen by all is a
greater good than that which is not, and that chosen by the ma-
1365ª jority than that chosen by the minority. For that which *all* desire
is good, as we have said; and so, the more a thing is desired, the
better it is. Further, that is the better thing which is considered so
by competitors or enemies, or, again, by authorized judges or
those whom they select to represent them. In the first two cases
the decision is virtually that of every one, in the last two that of authorities and experts. And sometimes it may be argued that what
5 all share is the better thing, since it is a dishonour not to share in
it; at other times, that what none or few share is better, since it is
rarer. The more praiseworthy things are, the nobler and therefore
the better they are. So with the things that earn greater honours
than others—honour is, as it were, a measure of value; and the
things whose absence involves comparatively heavy penalties; and
the things that are better than others admitted or believed to be
10 good. Moreover, things look better merely by being divided into
their parts, since they then seem to surpass a greater number of
things than before. Hence Homer says that Meleager was roused
to battle by the thought of

All horrors that light on a folk whose city is ta'en of their foes,
When they slaughter the men, when the burg is wasted with ravening
     flame,
15 When strangers are haling young children to thraldom, (fair women to
     shame).

The same effect is produced by piling up facts in a climax after the
manner of Epicharmus. The reason is partly the same as in the
case of division (for combination too makes the impression of
great superiority), and partly that the original thing appears to be
the cause and origin of important results. And since a thing is better when it is harder or rarer than other things, its superiority may
20 be due to seasons, ages, places, times, or one's natural powers.
When a man accomplishes something beyond his natural power,
or beyond his years, or beyond the measure of people like him, or
in a special way, or at a special place or time, his deed will have a
high degree of nobleness, goodness, and justice, or of their oppo-

sites. Hence the epigram on the victor at the Olympic games: 25

In time past, bearing a Yoke on my shoulders, of wood unshaven,
I carried my loads of fish from Argos to Tegea town.

So Iphicrates used to extol himself by describing the low estate
from which he had risen. Again, what is natural is better than what
is acquired, since it is harder to come by. Hence the words of
Homer:

I have learnt from none but myself. 30

And the best part of a good thing is particularly good; as when
Pericles in his funeral oration said that the country's loss of its
young men in battle was 'as if the spring were taken out of the
year'. So with those things which are of service when the need is
pressing; for example, in old age and times of sickness. And of two
things that which leads more directly to the end in view is the better. So too is that which is better for people generally as well as for
a particular individual. Again, what *can* be got is better than what 35
cannot, for it is good in a given case and the other thing is not.
And what is at the end of life is better than what is not, since those
things are ends in a greater degree which are nearer the end. What
aims at reality is better than what aims at appearance. We may de- 1365ᵇ
fine what aims at appearance as what a man will not choose if nobody is to know of his having it. This would seem to show that to
receive benefits is more desirable than to confer them, since a
man will choose the former even if nobody is to know of it, but it
is not the general view that he will choose the latter if nobody
knows of it. What a man wants to *be* is better than what a man 5
wants to *seem*, for in aiming at that he is aiming more at reality.
Hence men say that justice is of small value, since it is more desirable to seem just than to be just, whereas with health it is not
so. That is better than other things which is more useful than they
are for a number of different purposes; for example, that which
promotes life, good life, pleasure, and noble conduct. For this reason wealth and health are commonly thought to be of the highest 10
value, as possessing all these advantages. Again, that is better than
other things which is accompanied both with less pain and with
actual pleasure; for here there is more than one advantage; and so
here we have the good of feeling pleasure and also the good of not
feeling pain. And of two good things that is the better whose addition to a third thing makes a better whole than the addition of the
other to the same thing will make. Again, those things which we
are seen to possess are better than those which we are not seen to 15

possess, since the former have the air of reality. Hence wealth may
be regarded as a greater good if its existence is known to others.
That which is dearly prized is better than what is not—the sort of
thing that some people have only one of, though others have more
like it. Accordingly, blinding a one-eyed man inflicts worse injury
than half-blinding a man with two eyes; for the one-eyed man has
been robbed of what he dearly prized.

20   The grounds on which we must base our arguments, when we
are speaking for or against a proposal, have now been set forth
more or less completely.

Chapter 8

The most important and effective qualification for success in persuading audiences and speaking well on public affairs is to understand all the forms of government and to discriminate their
25 respective customs, institutions, and interests. For all men are persuaded by considerations of their interest, and their interest lies in
the maintenance of the established order. Further, it rests with the
supreme authority to give authoritative decisions, and this varies
with each form of government; there are as many different
supreme authorities as there are different forms of government.
The forms of government are four—democracy, oligarchy, aris-
30 tocracy, monarchy. The supreme right to judge and decide always
rests, therefore, with either a part or the whole of one or other of
these governing powers.

A Democracy is a form of government under which the citizens
distribute the offices of state among themselves by lot, whereas
under oligarchy there is a property qualification, under aristocracy
one of education. By education I mean that education which is
35 laid down by the law; for it is those who have been loyal to the national institutions that hold office under an aristocracy. These are
bound to be looked upon as 'the best men', and it is from this fact
that this form of government has derived its name ('the rule of the
best'). Monarchy, as the word implies, is the constitution in which
1366ª one man has authority over all. There are two forms of monarchy:
kingship, which is limited by prescribed conditions, and 'tyranny',
which is not limited by anything.

We must also notice the ends which the various forms of government pursue, since people choose in practice such actions as
will lead to the realization of their ends. The end of democracy is
freedom; of oligarchy, wealth; of aristocracy, the maintenance of

education and national institutions; of tyranny, the protection of
the tyrant. It is clear, then, that we must distinguish those particular customs, institutions, and interests which tend to realize the
ideal of each constitution, since men choose their means with reference to their ends. But rhetorical persuasion is effected not only
by demonstrative but by ethical argument; it helps a speaker to
convince us, if we believe that he has certain qualities himself,
namely, goodness, or goodwill towards us, or both together.
Similarly, we should know the moral qualities characteristic of
each form of government, for the special moral character of each
is bound to provide us with our most effective means of persuasion
in dealing with it. We shall learn the qualities of governments in
the same way as we learn the qualities of individuals, since they
are revealed in their deliberate acts of choice; and these are determined by the end that inspires them.

We have now considered the objects, immediate or distant, at
which we are to aim when urging any proposal, and the grounds
on which we are to base our arguments in favour of its utility. We
have also briefly considered the means and methods by which we
shall gain a good knowledge of the moral qualities and institutions
peculiar to the various forms of government—only, however, to
the extent demanded by the present occasion; a detailed account
of the subject has been given in the *Politics*.

Chapter 9

We have now to consider Virtue and Vice, the Noble and the
Base, since these are the objects of praise and blame. In doing so,
we shall at the same time be finding out how to make our hearers
take the required view of our own characters—our second method
of persuasion. The ways in which to make them trust the goodness
of other people are also the ways in which to make them trust our
own. Praise, again, may be serious or frivolous; nor is it always of
a human or divine being but often of inanimate things, or of the
humblest of the lower animals. Here too we must know on what
grounds to argue, and must, therefore, now discuss the subject,
though by way of illustration only.

The Noble is that which is both desirable for its own sake and
also worthy of praise; or that which is both good and also pleasant
because good. If this is a true definition of the Noble, it follows
that virtue must be noble, since it is both a good thing and also
praiseworthy. Virtue is, according to the usual view, a faculty of

providing and preserving good things; or a faculty of conferring many great benefits, and benefits of all kinds on all occasions. The 1366ᵇ forms of Virtue are justice, courage, temperance, magnificence, magnanimity, liberality, gentleness, prudence, wisdom. If virtue is a faculty of beneficence, the highest kinds of it must be those which are most useful to others, and for this reason men honour 5 most the just and the courageous, since courage is useful to others in war, justice both in war and in peace. Next comes liberality; liberal people let their money go instead of fighting for it, whereas other people care more for money than for anything else. Justice is the virtue through which everybody enjoys his own possessions 10 in accordance with the law; its opposite is injustice, through which men enjoy the possessions of others in defiance of the law. Courage is the virtue that disposes men to do noble deeds in situations of danger, in accordance with the law and in obedience to its commands; cowardice is the opposite. Temperance is the virtue 15 that disposes us to obey the law where physical pleasures are concerned; incontinence is the opposite. Liberality disposes us to spend money for others' good; illiberality is the opposite. Magnanimity is the virtue that disposes us to do good to others on a large scale; [its opposite is meanness of spirit]. Magnificence is a virtue productive of greatness in matters involving the spending of money. The opposites of these two are smallness of spirit and 20 meanness respectively. Prudence is that virtue of the understanding which enables men to come to wise decisions about the relation to happiness of the goods and evils that have been previously mentioned.

The above is a sufficient account, for our present purpose, of virtue and vice in general, and of their various forms. As to further 25 aspects of the subject, it is not difficult to discern the facts; it is evident that things productive of virtue are noble, as tending towards virtue; and also the effects of virtue, that is, the signs of its presence and the acts to which it leads. And since the signs of virtue, and such acts as it is the mark of a virtuous man to do or have done to 30 him, are noble, it follows that all deeds or signs of courage, and everything done courageously, must be noble things; and so with what is just and actions done justly. (Not, however, actions justly done to us; here justice is unlike the other virtues; 'justly' does not always mean 'nobly'; when a man is punished, it is more shameful that this should be justly than unjustly done to him). The same 35 is true of the other virtues. Again, those actions are noble for which the reward is simply honour, or honour more than money. So are those in which a man aims at something desirable for some one else's sake; actions good absolutely, such as those a man does for his country without thinking of himself; actions good in their own nature; actions that are not good simply for the individual, since individual interests are selfish. Noble also are those actions whose advantage may be enjoyed after death, as opposed to those 1367ᵃ whose advantage is enjoyed during one's lifetime: for the latter are more likely to be for one's own sake only. Also, all actions done for the sake of others, since these less than other actions are done for one's own sake; and all successes which benefit others and not oneself; and services done to one's benefactors, for this is just; and good deeds generally, since they are not directed to one's own profit. And the opposites of those things of which men feel ashamed, for men are ashamed of saying, doing, or intending to do shameful things. So when Alcaeus said

> Something I fain would say to thee,
> Only shame restraineth me,

Sappho wrote

> If for things good and noble thou wert yearning,
> If to speak baseness were thy tongue not burning,
> No load of shame would on thine eyelids weigh;
> What thou with honour wishest thou wouldst say.

Those things, also, are noble for which men strive anxiously, without feeling fear; for they feel thus about the good things which lead to fair fame. Again, one quality or action is nobler than another if it is that of a naturally finer being: thus a man's will be nobler than a woman's. And those qualities are noble which give more pleasure to other people than to their possessors; hence the nobleness of justice and just actions. It is noble to avenge oneself on one's enemies and not to come to terms with them; for requital is just, and the just is noble; and not to surrender is a sign of courage. Victory, too, and honour belong to the class of noble things, since they are desirable even when they yield no fruits, and they prove our superiority in good qualities. Things that deserve to be remembered are noble, and the more they deserve this, the nobler they are. So are the things that continue even after death; those which are always attended by honour; those which are exceptional; and those which are possessed by one person alone — these last are more readily remembered than others. So again are possessions that bring no profit, since they are more fitting than others for a gentleman. So are the distinctive qualities of a particular people, and the symbols of what it specially admires, like long

hair in Sparta, where this is a mark of a free man, as it is not easy
30   to perform any menial task when one's hair is long. Again, it is
noble not to practise any sordid craft, since it is the mark of a free
man not to live at another's beck and call. We are also to assume,
when we wish either to praise a man or blame him, that qualities
closely allied to those which he actually has are identical with
them; for instance, that the cautious man is cold-blooded and
35   treacherous, and that the stupid man is an honest fellow or the
thick-skinned man a good-tempered one. We can always idealize
any given man by drawing on the virtues akin to his actual qualities; thus we may say that the passionate and excitable man is 'outspoken'; or that the arrogant man is 'superb' or 'impressive'. Those
1367ᵇ who run to extremes will be said to possess the corresponding
good qualities; rashness will be called courage, and extravagance
generosity. That will be what most people think; and at the same
time this method enables an advocate to draw a misleading inference from the motive, arguing that if a man runs into danger
5   needlessly, much more will he do so in a noble cause; and if a
man is open-handed to any one and every one, he will be so to his
friends also, since it is the extreme form of goodness to be good to
everybody.

We must also take into account the nature of our particular audience when making a speech of praise; for, as Socrates used to
say, it is not difficult to praise the Athenians to an Athenian audience. If the audience esteems a given quality, we must say that our
10   hero has that quality, no matter whether we are addressing
Scythians or Spartans or philosophers. Everything, in fact, that is
esteemed we are to represent as noble. After all, people regard the
two things as much the same.

All actions are noble that are appropriate to the man who
does them: if, for instance, they are worthy of his ancestors or of
his own past career. For it makes for happiness, and is a noble
15   thing, that he should add to the honour he already has. Even inappropriate actions are noble if they are better and nobler than
the appropriate ones would be; for instance, if one who was just
an average person when all went well becomes a hero in adver-
sity, or if he becomes better and easier to get on with the higher
he rises. Compare the saying of Iphicrates, 'Think what I was
and what I am'; and the epigram on the victor at the Olympic
games,

In time past, bearing a yoke on my shoulders, of wood unshaven;

and the encomium of Simonides,

A woman whose father, whose husband, whose brethren were princes all.   20

Since we praise a man for what he has actually done, and fine
actions are distinguished from others by being intentionally good,
we must try to prove that our hero's noble acts are intentional.
This is all the easier if we can make out that he has often acted so
before, and therefore we must assert coincidences and accidents to
have been intended. Produce a number of good actions, all of the   25
same kind, and people will think that they must have been intended, and that they prove the good qualities of the man who did
them.

Praise is the expression in words of the eminence of a man's
good qualities, and therefore we must display his actions as the
product of such qualities. Encomium refers to what he has actually done; the mention of accessories, such as good birth and
education, merely helps to make our story credible—good fa-   30
thers are likely to have good sons, and good training is likely
to produce good character. Hence it is only when a man has
already done something that we bestow *encomiums* upon him.
Yet the actual deeds are evidence of the doer's character: even
if a man has not actually done a given good thing, we shall bestow *praise* on him, if we are sure that he is the sort of man
who *would* do it. To call any one blest is, it may be added, the
same thing as to call him happy; but these are not the same
thing as to bestow praise and encomium upon him; the two
latter are a part of 'calling happy', just as goodness is a part of   35
happiness.

To praise a man is in one respect akin to urging a course of action. The suggestions which would be made in the latter case become encomiums when differently expressed. When we know   1368ᵃ
what action or character is required, then, in order to express
these facts as suggestions for action, we have to change and reverse our form of words. Thus the statement 'A man should be
proud not of what he owes to fortune but of what he owes to himself', if put like this, amounts to a suggestion; to make it into   5
praise we must put it thus, 'Since he is proud not of what he owes
to fortune but of what he owes to himself.' Consequently, whenever you want to praise any one, think what you would urge people to do; and when you want to urge the doing of anything, think
what you would praise a man for having done. Since suggestion
may or may not forbid an action, the praise into which we con-
vert it must have one or other of two opposite forms of expression
accordingly.

10   There are, also, many useful ways of heightening the effect of praise. We must, for instance, point out that a man is the only one, or the first, or almost the only one who has done something, or that he has done it better than any one else; all these distinctions are honourable. And we must, further, make much of the particular season and occasion of an action, arguing that we could hardly have looked for it just then. If a man has often achieved the same success, we must mention this; that is a
15 strong point; he himself, and not luck, will then be given the credit. So, too, if it is on his account that observances have been devised and instituted to encourage or honour such achievements as his own: thus we may praise Hippolochus because the first encomium ever made was for him, or Harmodius and Aristogeiton because their statues were the first to be put up in the market-place. And we may censure bad men for the opposite reason.

    Again, if you cannot find enough to say of a man himself, you
20 may pit him against others, which is what Isocrates used to do owing to his want of familiarity with forensic pleading. The comparison should be with famous men; that will strengthen your case; it is a noble thing to surpass men who are themselves great. It is only natural that methods of 'heightening the effect' should be attached particularly to speeches of praise; they aim at proving superiority over others, and any such superiority is a form of nobleness. Hence if you cannot compare your hero with famous
25 men, you should at least compare him with other people generally, since any superiority is held to reveal excellence. And, in general, of the lines of argument which are common to all speeches, this 'heightening of effect' is most suitable for declamations, where we take our hero's actions as admitted facts, and our business is simply to invest these with dignity and nobility. 'Examples'
30 are most suitable to deliberative speeches; for we judge of future events by divination from past events. Enthymemes are most suitable to forensic speeches; it is our doubts about past events that most admit of arguments showing why a thing must have happened or proving that it did happen.

    The above are the general lines on which all, or nearly all, speeches of praise or blame are constructed. We have seen the sort of thing we must bear in mind in making such speeches, and the
35 materials out of which encomiums and censures are made. No special treatment of censure and vituperation is needed. Knowing the above facts, we know their contraries; and it is out of these that speeches of censure are made.

Chapter 10

We have next to treat of Accusation and Defence, and to enumer- 1368^b
ate and describe the ingredients of the syllogisms used therein.
There are three things we must ascertain—first, the nature and
number of the incentives to wrongdoing; second, the state of mind
of wrongdoers; third, the kind of persons who are wronged, and   5
their condition. We will deal with these questions in order. But before that let us define the act of 'wrong-doing'.

We may describe 'wrong-doing' as injury voluntarily inflicted
contrary to law. 'Law' is either special or general. By special law I
mean that written law which regulates the life of a particular community; by general law, all those unwritten principles which are
supposed to be acknowledged everywhere. We do things 'voluntar-   10
ily' when we do them consciously and without constraint. (Not all
voluntary acts are deliberate, but all deliberate acts are conscious—
no one is ignorant of what he deliberately intends.) The causes of
our deliberately intending harmful and wicked acts contrary to law
are (1) vice, (2) lack of self-control. For the wrongs a man does to
others will correspond to the bad quality or qualities that he him-   15
self possesses. Thus it is the mean man who will wrong others
about money, the profligate in matters of physical pleasure, the ef-
feminate in matters of comfort, and the coward where danger is
concerned—his terror makes him abandon those who are involved
in the same danger. The ambitious man does wrong for the sake of
honour, the quick-tempered from anger, the lover of victory for the 20
sake of victory, the embittered man for the sake of revenge, the stupid man because he has misguided notions of right and wrong, the
shameless man because he does not mind what people think of
him; and so with the rest—any wrong that any one does to others
corresponds to his particular faults of character.

However, this subject has already been cleared up in part in our   25
discussion of the virtues and will be further explained later when
we treat of the emotions. We have now to consider the motives
and states of mind of wrongdoers, and to whom they do wrong.

Let us first decide what sort of things people are trying to get or
avoid when they set about doing wrong to others. For it is plain that
the prosecutor must consider, out of all the aims that can ever induce us to do wrong to our neighbours, how many, and which, af-   30
fect his adversary; while the defendant must consider how many,
and which, do *not* affect him. Now every action of every person either is or is not due to that person himself. Of those not due to himself some are due to chance, the others to necessity; of these latter,

35   again, some are due to compulsion, the others to nature.
     Consequently all actions that are not due to a man himself are due
1369ᵃ either to chance or to nature or to compulsion. All actions that *are*
     due to a man himself and caused by himself are due either to habit
     or to rational or irrational craving. Rational craving is a craving for
     good, i.e. a *wish*—nobody wishes for anything unless he thinks it
     good. Irrational craving is twofold, viz. anger and appetite.

5   Thus every action must be due to one or other of seven causes:
     chance, nature, compulsion, habit, reasoning, anger, or appetite.
     It is superfluous further to distinguish actions according to the
     doers' ages, moral states, or the like; it is of course true that, for in-
     stance, young men do have hot tempers and strong appetites; still,
10   it is not through youth that they act accordingly, but through
     anger or appetite. Nor, again, is action due to wealth or poverty; it
     is of course true that poor men, being short of money, do have an
     appetite for it, and that rich men, being able to command need-
     less pleasures, do have an appetite for such pleasures: but here,
     again, their actions will be *due* not to wealth or poverty but to ap-
15   petite. Similarly, with just men, and unjust men, and all others
     who are said to act in accordance with their moral qualities, their
     actions will really be due to one of the causes mentioned—either
     reasoning or emotion: due, indeed, sometimes to good disposi-
     tions and good emotions, and sometimes to bad; but that good
     qualities should be followed by good emotions, and bad by bad, is
20   merely an accessory fact—it is no doubt true that the temperate
     man, for instance, because he is temperate, *is* always and at once
     attended by healthy opinions and appetites in regard to pleasant
     things, and the intemperate man by unhealthy ones. So we must
     ignore such distinctions. Still we must consider what kinds of ac-
     tions and of people usually go together; for while there are no def-
25   inite kinds of action associated with the fact that a man is fair or
     dark, tall or short, it does make a difference if he is young or old,
     just or unjust. And, generally speaking, all those accessory quali-
     ties that cause distinctions of human character are important: e.g.
     the sense of wealth or poverty, of being lucky or unlucky. This
30   shall be dealt with later—let us now deal first with the rest of the
     subject before us.

         The things that happen by chance are all those whose cause
     cannot be determined, that have no purpose, and that happen nei-
     ther always nor usually nor in any fixed way. The definition of
35   chance shows just what they are. Those things happen by nature
1369ᵇ which have a fixed and internal cause; they take place uniformly,
     either always or usually. There is no need to discuss in exact detail

the things that happen contrary to nature, nor to ask whether they
happen in some sense naturally or from some other cause; it
would seem that chance is at least partly the cause of such events.
Those things happen through compulsion which take place con-   5
trary to the desire or reason of the doer, yet through his own
agency. Acts are done from habit which men do because they
have often done them before. Actions are due to reasoning when,
in view of any of the goods already mentioned, they appear useful
either as ends or as means to an end, and are performed for that
reason: 'for that reason,' since even licentious persons perform a
certain number of useful actions, but because they are pleasant   10
and not because they are useful. To passion and anger are due all
acts of revenge. Revenge and punishment are different things.
Punishment is inflicted for the sake of the person punished; revenge for that of the punisher, to satisfy his feelings. (What anger
is will be made clear when we come to discuss the emotions.)
Appetite is the cause of all actions that appear pleasant. Habit,   15
whether acquired by mere familiarity or by effort, belongs to the
class of pleasant things, for there are many actions not naturally
pleasant which men perform with pleasure, once they have become used to them. To sum up then, all actions due to ourselves
either are or seem to be either good or pleasant. Moreover, as all   20
actions due to ourselves are done voluntarily and actions not due
to ourselves are done involuntarily, it follows that all voluntary actions must either be or seem to be either good or pleasant; for I
reckon among goods escape from evils or apparent evils and the
exchange of a greater evil for a less (since these things are in a   25
sense positively desirable), and likewise I count among pleasures
escape from painful or apparently painful things and the exchange
of a greater pain for a less. We must ascertain, then, the number
and nature of the things that are useful and pleasant. The useful
has been previously examined in connexion with political oratory;
let us now proceed to examine the pleasant. Our various defini-   30
tions must be regarded as adequate, even if they are not exact, provided they are clear.

Chapter 11

We may lay it down that Pleasure is a movement, a movement by
which the soul as a whole is consciously brought into its normal
state of being; and that Pain is the opposite. If this is what pleasure   1370ᵃ
is, it is clear that the pleasant is what tends to produce this condi-

tion, while that which tends to destroy it, or to cause the soul to be brought into the opposite state, is painful. It must therefore be pleasant as a rule to move towards a natural state of being, particularly when a natural process has achieved the complete recovery
5 of that natural state. Habits also are pleasant; for as soon as a thing has become habitual, it is virtually natural; habit is a thing not unlike nature; what happens often is akin to what happens always, natural events happening always, habitual events often. Again, that is pleasant which is not forced on us; for force is unnatural,
10 and that is why what is compulsory is painful, and it has been rightly said

All that is done on compulsion is bitterness unto the soul.

So all acts of concentration, strong effort, and strain are necessarily painful; they all involve compulsion and force, unless we are accustomed to them, in which case it is custom that makes them
15 pleasant. The opposites to these are pleasant; and hence ease, freedom from toil, relaxation, amusement, rest, and sleep belong to the class of pleasant things; for these are all free from any element of compulsion. Everything, too, is pleasant for which we have the desire within us, since desire is the craving for pleasure. Of the desires some are irrational, some associated with reason. By irrational I mean those which do not arise from any opinion held by
20 the mind. Of this kind are those known as 'natural'; for instance, those originating in the body, such as the desire for nourishment, namely hunger and thirst, and a separate kind of desire answering to each kind of nourishment; and the desires connected with taste and sex and sensations of touch in general; and those of smell,
25 hearing, and vision. Rational desires are those which we are induced to have; there are many things we desire to see or get because we have been told of them and induced to believe them good. Further, pleasure is the consciousness through the senses of a certain kind of emotion; but imagination is a feeble sort of sensation, and there will always be in the mind of a man who re-
30 members or expects something an image or picture of what he remembers or expects. If this is so, it is clear that memory and expectation also, being accompanied by sensation, may be accompanied by pleasure. It follows that anything pleasant is either present and perceived, past and remembered, or future and expected, since we perceive present pleasures, remember past ones,
1370ᵇ and expect future ones. Now the things that are pleasant to remember are not only those that, when actually perceived as present, *were* pleasant, but also some things that were not, provided

that their results have subsequently proved noble and good.
Hence the words

> Sweet 'tis when rescued to remember pain,

and

> Even his griefs are a joy long after to one that remembers   5
> All that he wrought and endured.

The reason of this is that it is pleasant even to be merely free from
evil. The things it is pleasant to expect are those that when present
are felt to afford us either great delight or great but not painful benefit. And in general, all the things that delight us when they are present also do so, as a rule, when we merely remember or expect them.   10
Hence even being angry is pleasant—Homer said of wrath that

> Sweeter it is by far than the honeycomb dripping with sweetness—

for no one grows angry with a person on whom there is no
prospect of taking vengeance, and we feel comparatively little
anger, or none at all, with those who are much our superiors in
power. Some pleasant feeling is associated with most of our ap-   15
petites; we are enjoying either the memory of a past pleasure or
the expectation of a future one, just as persons down with fever,
during their attacks of thirst, enjoy remembering the drinks they
have had and looking forward to having more. So also a lover enjoys talking or writing about his loved one, or doing any little thing   20
connected with him; all these things recall him to memory and
make him actually present to the eye of imagination. Indeed, it is
always the first sign of love, that besides enjoying some one's presence, we remember him when he is gone, and feel pain as well as
pleasure, because he is there no longer. Similarly there is an
element of pleasure even in mourning and lamentation for the de-   25
parted. There is grief, indeed, at his loss, but pleasure in remembering him and as it were seeing him before us in his deeds and
in his life. We can well believe the poet when he says

> He spake, and in each man's heart he awakened the love of lament.

Revenge, too, is pleasant; it is pleasant to get anything that it is
painful to fail to get, and angry people suffer extreme pain when   30
they fail to get their revenge; but they enjoy the prospect of getting
it. Victory also is pleasant, and not merely to 'bad losers', but to
every one; the winner sees himself in the light of a champion, and
everybody has a more or less keen appetite for being that. The
pleasantness of victory implies of course that combative sports and

1371ᵃ intellectual contests are pleasant (since in these it often happens
that some one wins) and also games like knucklebones, ball, dice,
and draughts. And similarly with the serious sports; some of these
become pleasant when one is accustomed to them: while others
are pleasant from the first, like hunting with hounds, or indeed
5   any kind of hunting. For where there is competition, there is victory. That is why forensic pleading and debating contests are pleasant to those who are accustomed to them and have the capacity
for them. Honour and good repute are among the most pleasant
things of all; they make a man see himself in the character of a
10   fine fellow, especially when he is credited with it by people whom
he thinks good judges. His neighbours are better judges than people at a distance; his associates and fellow-countrymen better than
strangers; his contemporaries better than posterity; sensible persons better than foolish ones; a large number of people better than
a small number: those of the former class, in each case, are the
more likely to be good judges of him. Honour and credit bestowed
15   by those whom you think much inferior to yourself—e.g. children
or animals—you do not value: not for its own sake, anyhow: if you
do value it, it is for some other reason. Friends belong to the class
of pleasant things; it is pleasant to love—if you love wine, you certainly find it delightful: and it is pleasant to be loved, for this too
20   makes a man see himself as the possessor of goodness, a thing that
every being that has a feeling for it desires to possess: to be loved
means to be valued for one's own personal qualities. To be admired is also pleasant, simply because of the honour implied.
Flattery and flatterers are pleasant: the flatterer is a man who, you
believe, admires and likes you. To do the same thing often is pleas-
25   ant, since, as we saw, anything habitual is pleasant. And to change
is also pleasant: change means an approach to nature, whereas invariable repetition of anything causes the excessive prolongation
of a settled condition: therefore, says the poet,

> Change is in all things sweet.

That is why what comes to us only at long intervals is pleasant,
whether it be a person or a thing; for it is a change from what we
30   had before, and, besides, what comes only at long intervals has the
value of rarity. Learning things and wondering at things are also
pleasant as a rule; wondering implies the desire of learning, so that
the object of wonder is an object of desire; while in learning one
is brought into one's natural condition. Conferring and receiving
benefits belong to the class of pleasant things; to receive a benefit
1371ᵇ is to get what one desires; to confer a benefit implies both posses-

sion and superiority, both of which are things we try to attain. It is because beneficent acts are pleasant that people find it pleasant to put their neighbours straight again and to supply what they lack. Again, since learning and wondering are pleasant, it follows that such things as acts of imitation must be pleasant—for instance, painting, sculpture, poetry—and every product of skilful imitation; this latter, even if the object imitated is not itself pleasant; for it is not the object itself which here gives delight; the spectator draws inferences ('That is a so-and-so') and thus learns something fresh. Dramatic turns of fortune and hairbreadth escapes from perils are pleasant, because we feel all such things are wonderful.

And since what is natural is pleasant, and things akin to each other seem natural to each other, therefore all kindred and similar things are usually pleasant to each other; for instance, one man, horse, or young person is pleasant to another man, horse, or young person. Hence the proverbs 'mate delights mate', 'like to like', 'beast knows beast', 'jackdaw to jackdaw', and the rest of them. But since everything like and akin to oneself is pleasant, and since every man is himself more like and akin to himself than any one else is, it follows that all of us must be more or less fond of ourselves. For all this resemblance and kinship is present particularly in the relation of an individual to himself. And because we are all fond of ourselves, it follows that what is our own is pleasant to all of us, as for instance our own deeds and words. That is why we are usually fond of our flatterers, [our lovers,] and honour; also of our children, for our children are our own work. It is also pleasant to complete what is defective, for the whole thing thereupon becomes our own work. And since power over others is very pleasant, it is pleasant to be thought wise, for practical wisdom secures us power over others. (Scientific wisdom is also pleasant, because it is the knowledge of many wonderful things.) Again, since most of us are ambitious, it must be pleasant to disparage our neighbours as well as to have power over them. It is pleasant for a man to spend his time over what he feels he can do best; just as the poet says,

> To that he bends himself,
> To that each day allots most time, wherein
> He is indeed the best part of himself.

Similarly, since amusement and every kind of relaxation and laughter too belong to the class of pleasant things, it follows that ludicrous things are pleasant, whether men, words, or deeds. We have discussed the ludicrous separately in the treatise on the *Art of Poetry*. 1372ᵃ

So much for the subject of pleasant things: by considering their opposites we can easily see what things are unpleasant.

Chapter 12

The above are the motives that make men do wrong to others; we are next to consider the states of mind in which they do it, and the persons to whom they do it.

They must themselves suppose that the thing can be done, and done by them: either that they can do it without being found out, or that if they are found out they can escape being punished, or that if they are punished the disadvantage will be less than the gain for themselves or those they care for. The general subject of apparent possibility and impossibility will be handled later on, since it is relevant not only to forensic but to all kinds of speaking. But it may here be said that people think that they can themselves most easily do wrong to others without being punished for it if they possess eloquence, or practical ability, or much legal experience, or a large body of friends, or a great deal of money. Their confidence is greatest if they personally possess the advantages mentioned: but even without them they are satisfied if they have friends or supporters or partners who do possess them: they can thus both commit their crimes and escape being found out and punished for committing them. They are also safe, they think, if they are on good terms with their victims or with the judges who try them. Their victims will in that case not be on their guard against being wronged, and will make some arrangement with them instead of prosecuting; while their judges will favour them because they like them, either letting them off altogether or imposing light sentences. They are not likely to be found out if their appearance contradicts the charges that might be brought against them: for instance, a weakling is unlikely to be charged with violent assault, or a poor and ugly man with adultery. Public and open injuries are the easiest to do, because nobody could at all suppose them possible, and therefore no precautions are taken. The same is true of crimes so great and terrible that no man living could be suspected of them: here too no precautions are taken. For all men guard against ordinary offences, just as they guard against ordinary diseases; but no one takes precautions against a disease that nobody has ever had. You feel safe, too, if you have either no enemies or a great many; if you have none, you expect not to be watched and therefore not to be detected; if you have a great

many, you will be watched, and therefore people will think you   30
can never risk an attempt on them, and you can defend your innocence by pointing out that you could never have taken such a
risk. You may also trust to hide your crime by the way you do it or
the place you do it in, or by some convenient means of disposal.

You may feel that even if you are found out you can stave off a
trial, or have it postponed, or corrupt your judges: or that even if
you are sentenced you can avoid paying damages, or can at least   35
postpone doing so for a long time: or that you are so badly off that
you will have nothing to lose. You may feel that the gain to be got
by wrong-doing is great or certain or immediate, and that the
penalty is small or uncertain or distant. It may be that the advan-   1372^b
tage to be gained is greater than any possible retribution: as in the
case of despotic power, according to the popular view. You may
consider your crimes as bringing you solid profit, while their punishment is nothing more than being called bad names. Or the opposite argument may appeal to you: your crimes may bring you
some credit (thus you may, incidentally, be avenging your father   5
or mother, like Zeno), whereas the punishment may amount to a
fine, or banishment, or something of that sort. People may be led
on to wrong others by either of these motives or feelings; but no
man by both—they will affect people of quite opposite characters.
You may be encouraged by having often escaped detection or
punishment already; or by having often tried and failed; for in   10
crime, as in war, there are men who will always refuse to give up
the struggle. You may get your pleasure on the spot and the pain
later, or the gain on the spot and the loss later. That is what appeals to weak-willed persons—and weakness of will may be shown
with regard to all the objects of desire. It may on the contrary appeal to you—as it does appeal to self-controlled and sensible
people—that the pain and loss are immediate, while the pleasure   15
and profit come later and last longer. You may feel able to make it
appear that your crime was due to chance, or to necessity, or to
natural causes, or to habit: in fact, to put it generally, as if you had
failed to do right rather than actually done wrong. You may be
able to trust other people to judge you equitably. You may be stim-
ulated by being in want: which may mean that you want neces-
saries, as poor people do, or that you want luxuries, as rich people   20
do. You may be encouraged by having a particularly good reputation, because that will save you from being suspected: or by having a particularly bad one, because nothing you are likely to do
will make it worse.

The above, then, are the various states of mind in which a man

sets about doing wrong to others. The kind of people to whom he does wrong, and the ways in which he does it, must be considered next. The people to whom he does it are those who have what he
25 wants himself, whether this means necessities or luxuries and materials for enjoyment. His victims may be far off or near at hand. If they are near, he gets his profit quickly; if they are far off, vengeance is slow, as those think who plunder the Carthaginians. They may be those who are trustful instead of being cautious and watchful, since all such people are easy to elude. Or those who are
30 too easy-going to have enough energy to prosecute an offender. Or sensitive people, who are not apt to show fight over questions of money. Or those who have been wronged already by many people, and yet have not prosecuted; such men must surely be the proverbial 'Mysian prey'. Or those who have either never or often been wronged before; in neither case will they take precautions; if they have never been wronged they think they never will, and if they have often been wronged they feel that surely it cannot hap-
35 pen again. Or those whose character has been attacked in the past, or is exposed to attack in the future: they will be too much frightened of the judges to make up their minds to prosecute, nor can
1373ª they win their case if they do: this is true of those who are hated or unpopular. Another likely class of victim is those who their injurer can pretend have, themselves or through their ancestors or friends, treated badly, or intended to treat badly, the man himself, or his ancestors, or those he cares for; as the proverb says, 'wickedness needs but a pretext'. A man may wrong his enemies, because that is pleasant: he may equally wrong his friends, because that is easy.
5 Then there are those who have no friends, and those who lack eloquence and practical capacity; these will either not attempt to prosecute, or they will come to terms, or failing that they will lose their case. There are those whom it does not pay to waste time in waiting for trial or damages, such as foreigners and small farmers; they will settle for a trifle, and always be ready to leave off. Also
10 those who have themselves wronged others, either often, or in the same way as they are now being wronged themselves—for it is felt that next to no wrong is done to people when it is the same wrong as they have often themselves done to others: if, for instance, you assault a man who has been accustomed to behave with violence to others. So too with those who have done wrong to others, or
15 have meant to, or mean to, or are likely to do so; there is something fine and pleasant in wronging such persons, it seems as though almost no wrong were done. Also those by doing wrong to whom we shall be gratifying our friends, or those we admire or

love, or our masters, or in general the people by reference to whom we mould our lives. Also those whom we may wrong and yet be sure of equitable treatment. Also those against whom we have had any grievance, or any previous differences with them, as Callippus had when he behaved as he did to Dion: here too it seems as if almost no wrong were being done. Also those who are   20
on the point of being wronged by others if we fail to wrong them ourselves, since here we feel we have no time left for thinking the matter over. So Aenesidemus is said to have sent the 'cottabus' prize to Gelon, who had just reduced a town to slavery, because Gelon had got there first and forestalled his own attempt. Also those by wronging whom we shall be able to do many righteous acts; for we feel that we can then easily cure the harm done. Thus   25
Jason the Thessalian said that it is a duty to do some unjust acts in order to be able to do many just ones.

Among the kinds of wrong done to others are those that are done universally, or at least commonly: one expects to be forgiven for doing these. Also those that can easily be kept dark, as where things that can rapidly be consumed like eatables are concerned, or things that can easily be changed in shape, colour, or combi-   30
nation, or things that can easily be stowed away almost any-where—portable objects that you can stow away in small corners, or things so like others of which you have plenty already that no-body can tell the difference. There are also wrongs of a kind that shame prevents the victim speaking about, such as outrages done to the women in his household or to himself or to his sons. Also   35
those for which you would be thought very litigious to prosecute any one—trifling wrongs, or wrongs for which people are usually excused.

The above is a fairly complete account of the circumstances under which men do wrong to others, of the sort of wrongs they do, of the sort of persons to whom they do them, and of their reasons for doing them.

Chapter 13

It will now be well to make a complete classification of just and 1373ᵇ
unjust actions. We may begin by observing that they have been de-fined relatively to two kinds of law, and also relatively to two classes of persons. By the two kinds of law I mean particular law and universal law. Particular law is that which each community lays down and applies to its own members: this is partly written   5

and partly unwritten. Universal law is the law of nature. For there really is, as every one to some extent divines, a natural justice and injustice that is binding on all men, even on those who have no association or covenant with each other. It is this that Sophocles' Antigone clearly means when she says that the burial of Polyneices
10   was a just act in spite of the prohibition: she means that it was just by nature.

>   Not of to-day or yesterday it is,
>   But lives eternal: none can date its birth.

And so Empedocles, when he bids us kill no living creature, says
15   that doing this is not just for some people while unjust for others,

>   Nay, but, an all-embracing law, through the realms of the sky
>   Unbroken it stretcheth, and over the earth's immensity.

And as Alcidamas says in his Messeniac Oration. . . .

The actions that we ought to do or not to do have also been di-
20   vided into two classes as affecting either the whole community or some one of its members. From this point of view we can perform just or unjust acts in either of two ways—towards one definite person, or towards the community. The man who is guilty of adultery or assault is doing wrong to some definite person; the man who
25   avoids service in the army is doing wrong to the community.

Thus the whole class of unjust actions may be divided into two classes, those affecting the community, and those affecting one or more other persons. We will next, before going further, remind ourselves of what 'being wronged' means. Since it has already been settled that 'doing a wrong' must be intentional, 'being wronged' must consist in having an injury done to you by some one who *intends* to do it. In order to be wronged, a man must (1)
30   suffer actual harm, (2) suffer it against his will. The various possible forms of harm are clearly explained by our previous separate discussion of goods and evils. We have also seen that a voluntary action is one where the doer knows what he is doing. We now see that every accusation must be of an action affecting either the community or some individual. The doer of the action must either
35   understand and intend the action, or not understand and intend it. In the former case, he must be acting either from deliberate choice or from passion. (Anger will be discussed when we speak of the passions; the motives for crime and the state of mind of the
1374ᵃ   criminal have already been discussed.) Now it often happens that a man will admit an act, but will not admit the prosecutor's label for the act nor the facts which that label implies. He will admit

that he took a thing but not that he 'stole' it; that he struck some
one first, but not that he committed 'outrage'; that he had intercourse with a woman, but not that he committed 'adultery'; that
he is guilty of theft, but not that he is guilty of 'sacrilege', the object stolen not being consecrated; that he has encroached, but not
that he has 'encroached on State lands'; that he has been in com-   5
munication with the enemy, but not that he has been guilty of
'treason'. Here therefore we must be able to distinguish what is
theft, outrage, or adultery, from what is not, if we are to be able to
make the justice of our case clear, no matter whether our aim is
to establish a man's guilt or to establish his innocence. Wherever   10
such charges are brought against a man, the question is whether
he is or is not guilty of a criminal offence. It is deliberate purpose
that constitutes wickedness and criminal guilt, and such names as
'outrage' or 'theft' imply deliberate purpose as well as the mere action. A blow does not always amount to 'outrage', but only if it is
struck with some such purpose as to insult the man struck or gratify the striker himself. Nor does taking a thing without the owner's   15
knowledge always amount to 'theft', but only if it is taken with the
intention of keeping it and injuring the owner. And as with these
charges, so with all the others.

We saw that there are two kinds of right and wrong conduct towards others, one provided for by written ordinances, the other by
unwritten. We have now discussed the kind about which the laws   20
have something to say. The other kind has itself two varieties.
First, there is the conduct that springs from exceptional goodness
or badness, and is visited accordingly with censure and loss of honour, or with praise and increase of honour and decorations: for
instance, gratitude to, or requital of, our benefactors, readiness to
help our friends, and the like. The second kind makes up for the   25
defects of a community's written code of law. This is what we call
equity; people regard it as just; it is, in fact, the sort of justice
which goes beyond the written law. Its existence partly is and
partly is not intended by legislators; not intended, where they have
noticed no defect in the law; intended, where they find themselves unable to define things exactly, and are obliged to legislate   30
as if that held good always which in fact only holds good usually;
or where it is not easy to be complete owing to the endless possible cases presented, such as the kinds and sizes of weapons that
may be used to inflict wounds—a lifetime would be too short to
make out a complete list of these. If, then, a precise statement is
impossible and yet legislation is necessary, the law must be ex-   35
pressed in wide terms; and so, if a man has no more than a finger-

ring on his hand when he lifts it to strike or actually strikes another
man, he is guilty of a criminal act according to the written words
1374ᵇ of the law; but he is innocent really, and it is equity that declares
him to be so. From this definition of equity it is plain what sort of
actions, and what sort of persons, are equitable or the reverse.
Equity must be applied to forgivable actions; and it must make us
5   distinguish between criminal acts on the one hand, and errors of
judgement, or misfortunes, on the other. (A 'misfortune' is an act,
not due to moral badness, that has unexpected results: an 'error of
judgement' is an act, also not due to moral badness, that has results that might have been expected: a 'criminal act' has results
that might have been expected, but *is* due to moral badness, for
10   that is the source of all actions inspired by our appetites.) Equity
bids us be merciful to the weakness of human nature; to think less
about the laws than about the man who framed them, and less
about what he said than about what he meant; not to consider the
actions of the accused so much as his intentions; nor this or that
15   detail so much as the whole story; to ask not what a man is now
but what he has always or usually been. It bids us remember benefits rather than injuries, and benefits received rather than benefits conferred; to be patient when we are wronged; to settle a dis-
20   pute by negotiation and not by force; to prefer arbitration to liti-
gation—for an arbitrator goes by the equity of a case, a judge by
the strict law, and arbitration was invented with the express purpose of securing full power for equity.

The above may be taken as a sufficient account of the nature of
equity.

Chapter 14

The worse of two acts of wrong done to others is that which is
25   prompted by the worse disposition. Hence the most trifling acts
may be the worst ones; as when Callistratus charged Melanopus
with having cheated the temple-builders of three consecrated half-
obols. The converse is true of just acts. This is because the greater
is here potentially contained in the less: there is no crime that a
man who has stolen three consecrated half-obols would shrink
from committing. Sometimes, however, the worse act is reckoned
30   not in this way but by the greater harm that it does. Or it may be
because no punishment for it is severe enough to be adequate; or
the harm done may be incurable—a difficult and even hopeless
crime to defend; or the sufferer may not be able to get his injurer

legally punished, a fact that makes the harm incurable, since legal punishment and chastisement are the proper cure. Or again, the man who has suffered wrong may have inflicted some fearful punishment on himself; then the doer of the wrong ought in justice to receive a still more fearful punishment. Thus Sophocles, when 35 pleading for retribution to Euctemon, who had cut his own throat because of the outrage done to him, said he would not fix a 1375ª penalty less than the victim had fixed for himself. Again, a man's crime is worse if he has been the first man, or the only man, or almost the only man, to commit it: or if it is by no means the first time he has gone seriously wrong in the same way: or if his crime has led to the thinking-out and invention of measures to prevent and punish similar crimes—thus in Argos a penalty is inflicted on 5 a man on whose account a law is passed, and also on those on whose account the prison was built: or if a crime is specially brutal, or specially deliberate: or if the report of it awakes more terror than pity. There are also such rhetorically effective ways of putting it as the following: That the accused has disregarded and broken not one but many solemn obligations like oaths, promises, pledges, or rights of intermarriage between states—here the crime 10 is worse because it consists of many crimes; and that the crime was committed in the very place where criminals are punished, as for example perjurers do—it is argued that a man who will commit a crime in a law-court would commit it anywhere. Further, the worse deed is that which involves the doer in special shame; that whereby a man wrongs his benefactors—for he does more than one wrong, by not merely doing them harm but failing to do them 15 good; that which breaks the unwritten laws of justice—the better sort of man will be just without being forced to be so, and the written laws depend on force while the unwritten ones do not. It may however be argued otherwise, that the crime is worse which breaks the written laws: for the man who commits crimes for which terrible penalties are provided will not hesitate over crimes 20 for which no penalty is provided at all.—So much, then, for the comparative badness of criminal actions.

Chapter 15

There are also the so-called 'non-technical' means of persuasion; and we must now take a cursory view of these, since they are specially characteristic of forensic oratory. They are five in number: laws, witnesses, contracts, tortures, oaths.

25   First, then, let us take laws and see how they are to be used in
persuasion and dissuasion, in accusation and defence. If the written law tells against our case, clearly we must appeal to the universal law, and insist on its greater equity and justice. We must
argue that the juror's oath 'I will give my verdict according to my
30   honest opinion' means that one will not simply follow the letter of
the written law. We must urge that the principles of equity are per-
manent and changeless, and that the universal law does not
change either, for it is the law of nature, whereas written laws often
do change. This is the bearing of the lines in Sophocles' *Antigone*,
where Antigone pleads that in burying her brother she had broken
Creon's law, but not the unwritten law:

1375^b   Not of to-day or yesterday they are,
                  But live eternal: (none can date their birth.)
                  Not I would fear the wrath of any man,
                  (And brave God's vengeance) for defying these.

We shall argue that justice indeed is true and profitable, but that
sham justice is not, and that consequently the written law is not,
5   because it does not fulfil the true purpose of law. Or that justice is
like silver, and must be assayed by the judges, if the genuine is to
be distinguished from the counterfeit. Or that the better a man is,
the more he will follow and abide by the unwritten law in prefer-
ence to the written. Or perhaps that the law in question contradicts some other highly-esteemed law, or even contradicts itself.
Thus it may be that one law will enact that all contracts must be
10   held binding, while another forbids us ever to make illegal contracts. Or if a law is ambiguous, we shall turn it about and consider
which construction best fits the interests of justice or utility, and
then follow that way of looking at it. Or if, though the law still exists, the situation to meet which it was passed exists no longer, we
15   must do our best to prove this and to combat the law thereby. If
however the written law supports our case, we must urge that the
oath 'to give my verdict according to my honest opinion' is not
meant to make the judges give a verdict that is contrary to the law,
but to save them from the guilt of perjury if they misunderstand
what the law really means. Or that no one chooses what is absolutely good, but every one what is good for himself. Or that not
20   to use the laws is as bad as to have no laws at all. Or that, as in the
other arts, it does not pay to try to be cleverer than the doctor: for
less harm comes from the doctor's mistakes than from the growing
habit of disobeying authority. Or that trying to be cleverer than the
laws is just what is forbidden by those codes of law that are ac-

counted best.—So far as the laws are concerned, the above discussion is probably sufficient.   25

As to witnesses, they are of two kinds, the ancient and the recent; and these latter, again, either do or do not share in the risks
of the trial. By 'ancient' witnesses I mean the poets and all other
notable persons whose judgements are known to all. Thus the
Athenians appealed to Homer as a witness about Salamis; and the   30
men of Tenedos not long ago appealed to Periander of Corinth in
their dispute with the people of Sigeum; and Cleophon supported
his accusation of Critias by quoting the elegiac verse of Solon,
maintaining that discipline had long been slack in the family of
Critias, or Solon would never have written,

Pray thee, bid the red-haired Critias do what his father commands him.

These witnesses are concerned with past events. As to future
events we shall also appeal to soothsayers: thus Themistocles   1376ᵃ
quoted the oracle about 'the wooden wall' as a reason for engag-
ing the enemy's fleet. Further, proverbs are, as has been said, one
form of evidence. Thus if you are urging somebody not to make a
friend of an old man, you will appeal to the proverb,

Never show an old man kindness.   5

Or if you are urging that he who has made away with fathers
should also make away with their sons, quote,

Fool, who slayeth the father and leaveth his sons to avenge him.

'Recent' witnesses are well-known people who have expressed
their opinions about some disputed matter: such opinions will be
useful support for subsequent disputants on the same points: thus
Eubulus used in the law-courts against Chares the reply Plato had   10
made to Archibius, 'It has become the regular custom in this
country to admit that one is a scoundrel'. There are also those witnesses who share the risk of punishment if their evidence is pronounced false. These are valid witnesses to the fact that an action
was or was not done, that something is or is not the case; they are   15
not valid witnesses to the quality of an action, to its being just or
unjust, useful or harmful. On such questions of *quality* the opinion of detached persons is highly trustworthy. Most trustworthy of
all are the 'ancient' witnesses, since they cannot be corrupted.

In dealing with the evidence of witnesses, the following are useful arguments. If you have no witnesses on your side, you will
argue that the judges must decide from what is probable; that this
is meant by 'giving a verdict in accordance with one's honest

20   opinion'; that probabilities cannot be bribed to mislead the court;
     and that probabilities are never convicted of perjury. If you *have*
     witnesses, and the other man has not, you will argue that proba-
     bilities cannot be put on their trial, and that we could do without
     the evidence of witnesses altogether if we need do no more than
     balance the pleas advanced on either side.

         The evidence of witnesses may refer either to ourselves or to our
     opponent; and either to questions of fact or to questions of per-
25   sonal character: so, clearly, we need never be at a loss for useful
     evidence. For if we have no evidence of fact supporting our own
     case or telling against that of our opponent, at least we can always
     find evidence to prove our own worth or our opponent's worth-
     lessness. Other arguments about a witness—that he is a friend or
30   an enemy or neutral, or has a good, bad, or indifferent reputation,
     and any other such distinctions—we must construct upon the
     same general lines as we use for the regular rhetorical proofs.

         Concerning contracts argument can be so far employed as to
     increase or diminish their importance and their credibility; we
1376ᵇ shall try to increase both if they tell in our favour, and to diminish
     both if they tell in favour of our opponent. Now for confirming or
     upsetting the credibility of contracts the procedure is just the same
     as for dealing with witnesses, for the credit to be attached to con-
     tracts depends upon the character of those who have signed them
     or have the custody of them. The contract being once admitted
     genuine, we must insist on its importance, if it supports our case.
     We may argue that a contract is a law, though of a special and lim-
     ited kind; and that, while contracts do not of course make the law
     binding, the law does make any lawful contract binding, and that
10   the law itself as a whole is a sort of contract, so that any one who
     disregards or repudiates any contract is repudiating the law itself.
     Further, most business relations—those, namely, that are vol-
     untary—are regulated by contracts, and if these lose their binding
     force, human intercourse ceases to exist. We need not go very
     deep to discover the other appropriate arguments of this kind. If,
15   however, the contract tells against us and for our opponents, in the
     first place those arguments are suitable which we can use to fight
     a law that tells against us. We do not regard ourselves as bound to
     observe a bad law which it was a mistake ever to pass: and it is
     ridiculous to suppose that we are bound to observe a bad and mis-
20   taken contract. Again, we may argue that the duty of the judge as
     umpire is to decide what is just, and therefore he must ask where
     justice lies, and not what this or that document means. And that
     it is impossible to pervert justice by fraud or by force, since it is

founded on nature, but a party to a contract may be the victim of
either fraud or force. Moreover, we must see if the contract con-
travenes either universal law or any written law of our own or   25
another country; and also if it contradicts any other previous or
subsequent contract; arguing that the subsequent is the binding
contract, or else that the previous one was right and the subsequent one fraudulent—whichever way suits us. Further, we must
consider the question of utility, noting whether the contract is
against the interest of the judges or not; and so on—these argu-   30
ments are as obvious as the others.

Examination by torture is one form of evidence, to which great
weight is often attached because it is in a sense compulsory. Here
again it is not hard to point out the available grounds for magnifying its value, if it happens to tell in our favour, and arguing that it
is the only form of evidence that is infallible; or, on the other
hand, for refuting it if it tells against us and for our opponent,   1377ᵃ
when we may say what is true of torture of every kind alike, that
people under its compulsion tell lies quite as often as they tell the
truth, sometimes persistently refusing to tell the truth, sometimes   5
recklessly making a false charge in order to be let off sooner. We
ought to be able to quote cases, familiar to the judges, in which
this sort of thing has actually happened. [We must say that evidence under torture is not trustworthy, the fact being that many
men whether thick-witted, tough-skinned, or stout of heart endure
their ordeal nobly, while cowards and timid men are full of bold-
ness till they see the ordeal of these others: so that no trust can be
placed in evidence under torture.]

In regard to oaths, a fourfold division can be made. A man may
either both offer and accept an oath, or neither, or one without the
other—that is, he may offer an oath but not accept one, or accept
an oath but not offer one. There is also the situation that arises   10
when an oath has already been sworn either by himself or by his
opponent.

If you refuse to offer an oath, you may argue that men do not
hesitate to perjure themselves; and that if your opponent does
swear, you lose your money, whereas, if he does not, you think the
judges will decide against him; and that the risk of an un-
favourable verdict is preferable, since you trust the judges and do   15
not trust him.

If you refuse to accept an oath, you may argue that an oath is
always paid for; that you would of course have taken it if you had
been a rascal, since if you *are* a rascal you had better make something by it, and you would in that case have to swear in order to

succeed. Thus your refusal, you argue, must be due to high principle, not to fear of perjury: and you may aptly quote the saying of
Xenophanes,

20   'Tis not fair that he who fears not God should challenge him who doth.

It is as if a strong man were to challenge a weakling to strike, or be
struck by, him.

If you agree to accept an oath, you may argue that you trust
yourself but not your opponent; and that (to invert the remark of
Xenophanes) the fair thing is for the impious man to offer the oath
and for the pious man to accept it; and that it would be monstrous
if you yourself were unwilling to accept an oath in a case where
25   you demand that the judges should do so before giving their verdict. If you wish to offer an oath, you may argue that piety disposes
you to commit the issue to the gods; and that your opponent ought
not to want other judges than himself, since you leave the decision
with him; and that it is outrageous for your opponents to refuse to
swear about this question, when they insist that others should do
so.

Now that we see how we are to argue in each case separately,
we see also how we are to argue when they occur in pairs, namely,
30   when you are willing to accept the oath but not to offer it; to offer
it but not to accept it; both to accept and to offer it; or to do nei-
1377ᵇ ther. These are of course combinations of the cases already mentioned, and so your arguments also must be combinations of the
arguments already mentioned.

If you have already sworn an oath that contradicts your present
one, you must argue that it is not perjury, since perjury is a crime,
and a crime must be a voluntary action, whereas actions due to
5   the force or fraud of others are involuntary. You must further reason from this that perjury depends on the intention and not on the
spoken words. But if it is your opponent who has already sworn an
oath that contradicts his present one, you must say that if he does
not abide by his oaths he is the enemy of society, and that this is
the reason why men take an oath before administering the laws.
'My opponents insist that you, the judges, must abide by the oath
10   you have sworn, and yet they are not abiding by their own oaths.'
And there are other arguments which may be used to magnify the
importance of the oath. — [So much, then, for the 'non-technical'
modes of persuasion.]

BOOK II

BOOK II

Chapter 1

WE have now considered the materials to be used in supporting or
opposing a political measure, in pronouncing eulogies or censures, and for prosecution and defence in the law courts. We have
considered the received opinions on which we may best base our
arguments so as to convince our hearers—those opinions with
which our enthymemes deal, and out of which they are built, in
each of the three kinds of oratory, according to what may be called   20
the special needs of each.

But since rhetoric exists to affect the giving of decisions—the
hearers decide between one political speaker and another, and a
legal verdict *is* a decision—the orator must not only try to make
the argument of his speech demonstrative and worthy of belief; he
must also make his own character look right and put his hearers,
who are to decide, into the right frame of mind. Particularly in political oratory, but also in lawsuits, it adds much to an orator's in-   25
fluence that his own character should look right and that he
should be thought to entertain the right feelings towards his hearers; and also that his hearers themselves should be in just the right
frame of mind. That the orator's own character should look right
is particularly important in political speaking: that the audience   30
should be in the right frame of mind, in lawsuits. When people
are feeling friendly and placable, they think one sort of thing;
when they are feeling angry or hostile, they think either something
totally different or the same thing with a different intensity: when   1378ª
they feel friendly to the man who comes before them for judgement, they regard him as having done little wrong, if any; when
they feel hostile, they take the opposite view. Again, if they are
eager for, and have good hopes of, a thing that will be pleasant
if it happens, they think that it certainly will happen and be good
for them: whereas if they are indifferent or annoyed, they do not   5
think so.

There are three things which inspire confidence in the orator's own character—the three, namely, that induce us to believe a thing apart from any proof of it: good sense, good moral character,
10   and goodwill. False statements and bad advice are due to one or more of the following three causes. Men either form a false opinion through want of good sense; or they form a true opinion, but because of their moral badness do not say what they really think; or finally, they are both sensible and upright, but not well disposed to their hearers, and may fail in consequence to recommend what they know to be the best course. These are the only possible cases.
15   It follows that any one who is thought to have all three of these good qualities will inspire trust in his audience. The way to make ourselves thought to be sensible and morally good must be gathered from the analysis of goodness already given: the way to establish your own goodness is the same as the way to establish that of others. Good will and friendliness of disposition will form part of our discussion of the emotions, to which we must now turn.
20   The Emotions are all those feelings that so change men as to affect their judgements, and that are also attended by pain or pleasure. Such are anger, pity, fear and the like, with their opposites. We must arrange what we have to say about each of them under three heads. Take, for instance, the emotion of anger: here we must discover (1) what the state of mind of angry people is, (2)
25   who the people are with whom they usually get angry, and (3) on what grounds they get angry with them. It is not enough to know one or even two of these points; unless we know all three, we shall be unable to arouse anger in any one. The same is true of the other emotions. So just as earlier in this work we drew up a list of
30   useful propositions for the orator, let us now proceed in the same way to analyse the subject before us.

Chapter 2

Anger may be defined as an impulse, accompanied by pain, to a conspicuous revenge for a conspicuous slight directed without justification towards what concerns oneself or towards what concerns one's friends. If this is a proper definition of anger, it must always be felt towards some particular individual, e.g. Cleon, and not 'man' in general. It must be felt because the other has done or in-
1378ᵇ tended to do something to him or one of his friends. It must always be attended by a certain pleasure—that which arises from the expectation of revenge. For since nobody aims at what he thinks he

cannot attain, the angry man is aiming at what he can attain, and
the belief that you will attain your aim is pleasant. Hence it has   5
been well said about wrath,

> Sweeter it is by far than the honeycomb dripping with sweetness,
> And spreads through the hearts of men.

It is also attended by a certain pleasure because the thoughts dwell
upon the act of vengeance, and the images then called up cause
pleasure, like the images called up in dreams.

Now slighting is the actively entertained opinion of something   10
as obviously of no importance. We think bad things, as well as
good ones, have serious importance; and we think the same of
anything that tends to produce such things, while those which
have little or no such tendency we consider unimportant. There
are three kinds of slighting—contempt, spite, and insolence. (1)
Contempt is one kind of slighting: you feel contempt for what you   15
consider unimportant, and it is just such things that you slight. (2)
Spite is another kind; it is a thwarting another man's wishes, not
to get something yourself but to prevent his getting it. The slight
arises just from the fact that you do not aim at something for yourself: clearly you do not think that he can do you harm, for then   20
you would be afraid of him instead of slighting him, nor yet that
he can do you any good worth mentioning, for then you would be
anxious to make friends with him. (3) Insolence is also a form of
slighting, since it consists in doing and saying things that cause
shame to the victim, not in order that anything may happen to
yourself, or because anything has happened to yourself, but sim-   25
ply for the pleasure involved. (Retaliation is not 'insolence', but
vengeance.) The cause of the pleasure thus enjoyed by the insolent man is that he thinks himself greatly superior to others when
ill-treating them. That is why youths and rich men are insolent;
they think themselves superior when they show insolence. One
sort of insolence is to rob people of the honour due to them; you
certainly slight them thus; for it is the unimportant, for good or   30
evil, that has no honour paid to it. So Achilles says in anger:

> He hath taken my prize for himself and hath done me dishonour,

and

> Like an alien honoured by none,

meaning that this is why he is angry. A man expects to be specially
respected by his inferiors in birth, in capacity, in goodness, and
generally in anything in which he is much their superior: as where   1379ᵃ

money is concerned a wealthy man looks for respect from a poor man; where speaking is concerned, the man with a turn for oratory looks for respect from one who cannot speak; the ruler demands the respect of the ruled, and the man who thinks he ought to be a ruler demands the respect of the man whom he thinks he ought to be ruling. Hence it has been said

> Great is the wrath of kings, whose father is Zeus almighty,

and

5   Yea, but his rancour abideth long afterward also,

their great resentment being due to their great superiority. Then again a man looks for respect from those who he thinks owe him good treatment, and these are the people whom he has treated or is treating well, or means or has meant to treat well, either himself, or through his friends, or through others at his request.

It will be plain by now, from what has been said, (1) in what frame of mind, (2) with what persons, and (3) on what grounds people grow angry. (1) The frame of mind is that in which any 10 pain is being felt. In that condition, a man is always aiming at something. Whether, then, another man opposes him either directly in any way, as by preventing him from drinking when he is thirsty, or indirectly, the act appears to him just the same; whether some one works against him, or fails to work with him, or otherwise vexes him while he is in this mood, he is equally angry in all 15 these cases. Hence people who are afflicted by sickness or poverty or love or thirst or any other unsatisfied desires are prone to anger and easily roused: especially against those who slight their present distress. Thus a sick man is angered by disregard of his illness, a poor man by disregard of his poverty, a man waging war by disregard of the war he is waging, a lover by disregard of his love, and 20 so throughout, any other sort of slight being enough if special slights are wanting. Each man is predisposed, by the emotion now controlling him, to his own particular anger. Further, we are angered if we happen to be expecting a contrary result: for a quite unexpected evil is specially painful, just as the quite unexpected fulfilment of our wishes is specially pleasant. Hence it is plain 25 what seasons, times, conditions, and periods of life tend to stir men easily to anger, and where and when this will happen; and it is plain that the more we are under these conditions the more easily we are stirred.

These, then, are the frames of mind in which men are easily stirred to anger. The persons with whom we get angry are those

who laugh, mock, or jeer at us, for such conduct is insolent. Also
those who inflict injuries upon us that are marks of insolence.   30
These injuries must be such as are neither retaliatory nor profitable to the doers: for only then will they be felt to be due to insolence. Also those who speak ill of us, and show contempt for us,
in connexion with the things we ourselves most care about: thus
those who are eager to win fame as philosophers get angry with
those who show contempt for their philosophy; those who pride   35
themselves upon their appearance get angry with those who show
contempt for their appearance; and so on in other cases. We feel
particularly angry on this account if we suspect that we are in fact,
or that people think we are, lacking completely or to an effective
extent in the qualities in question. For when we are convinced   1379ᵇ
that we excel in the qualities for which we are jeered at, we can ig-
nore the jeering. Again, we are angrier with our friends than with
other people, since we feel that our friends ought to treat us well
and not badly. We are angry with those who have usually treated
us with honour or regard, if a change comes and they behave to   5
us otherwise: for we think that they feel contempt for us, or they
would still be behaving as they did before. And with those who do
not return our kindnesses or fail to return them adequately, and
with those who oppose us though they are our inferiors: for all
such persons seem to feel contempt for us; those who oppose us
seem to think us inferior to themselves, and those who do not return our kindnesses seem to think that those kindnesses were conferred by inferiors. And we feel particularly angry with men of no
account at all, if they slight us. For, by our hypothesis, the anger   10
caused by the slight is felt towards people who are not justified in
slighting us, and our inferiors are not thus justified. Again, we feel
angry with friends if they do not speak well of us or treat us well;
and still more, if they do the contrary; or if they do not perceive
our needs, which is why Plexippus is angry with Meleager in
Antiphon's play; for this want of perception shows that they are   15
slighting us—we do not fail to perceive the needs of those for
whom we care. Again, we are angry with those who rejoice at our
misfortunes or simply keep cheerful in the midst of our misfortunes, since this shows that they either hate us or are slighting us.
Also with those who are indifferent to the pain they give us: this is
why we get angry with bringers of bad news. And with those who   20
listen to stories about us or keep on looking at our weaknesses; this
seems like either slighting us or hating us; for those who love us
share in all our distresses and it must distress any one to keep on
looking at his own weaknesses. Further, with those who slight us

before five classes of people: namely, (1) our rivals, (2) those
25 whom we admire, (3) those whom we wish to admire us, (4) those
for whom we feel reverence, (5) those who feel reverence for us:
if any one slights us before such persons, we feel particularly
angry. Again, we feel angry with those who slight us in connexion
with what we are as honourable men bound to champion—our
30 parents, children, wives, or subjects. And with those who do not
return a favour, since such a slight is unjustifiable. Also with those
who reply with humorous levity when we are speaking seriously,
for such behaviour indicates contempt. And with those who treat
us less well than they treat everybody else; it is another mark of
contempt that they should think we do not deserve what every one
35 else deserves. Forgetfulness, too, causes anger, as when our own
names are forgotten, trifling as this may be; since forgetfulness is
felt to be another sign that we are being slighted; it is due to neg-
ligence, and to neglect us is to slight us.

The persons with whom we feel anger, the frame of mind in
1380ª which we feel it, and the reasons why we feel it, have now all been
set forth. Clearly the orator will have to speak so as to bring his
hearers into a frame of mind that will dispose them to anger, and
to represent his adversaries as open to such charges and possessed
of such qualities as do make people angry.

Chapter 3

5   Since growing calm is the opposite of growing angry, and calm-
ness the opposite of anger, we must ascertain in what frames of
mind men are calm, towards whom they feel calm, and by what
means they are made so. Growing calm may be defined as a set-
tling down or quieting of anger. Now we get angry with those who
slight us; and since slighting is a voluntary act, it is plain that we
10 feel calm towards those who do nothing of the kind, or who do or
seem to do it involuntarily. Also towards those who intended to do
the opposite of what they did do. Also towards those who treat
themselves as they have treated us: since no one can be supposed
to slight himself. Also towards those who admit their fault and are
sorry: since we accept their grief at what they have done as satis-
15 faction, and cease to be angry. The punishment of servants shows
this: those who contradict us and deny their offence we punish all
the more, but we cease to be incensed against those who agree
that they deserved their punishment. The reason is that it is
shameless to deny what is obvious, and those who are shameless

towards us slight us and show contempt for us: anyhow, we do not 20
feel shame before those of whom we are thoroughly contemptuous. Also we feel calm towards those who humble themselves
before us and do not gainsay us; we feel that they thus admit themselves our inferiors, and inferiors feel fear, and nobody can slight
any one so long as he feels afraid of him. That our anger ceases towards those who humble themselves before us is shown even by 25
dogs, who do not bite people when they sit down. We also feel
calm towards those who are serious when we are serious, because
then we feel that we are treated seriously and not contemptuously.
Also towards those who have done us more kindnesses than we
have done them. Also towards those who pray to us and beg for
mercy, since they humble themselves by doing so. Also towards
those who do not insult or mock at or slight any one at all, or not 30
any worthy person or any one like ourselves. In general, the things
that make us calm may be inferred by seeing what the opposites
are of those that make us angry. We are not angry with people we
fear or respect, as long as we fear or respect them; you cannot be
afraid of a person and also at the same time angry with him. Again,
we feel no anger, or comparatively little, with those who have
done what they did through anger: we do not feel that they have 35
done it from a wish to slight us, for no one slights people when
angry with them, since slighting is painless, and anger is painful.
Nor do we grow angry with those who reverence us. 1380^b

As to the frame of mind that makes people calm, it is plainly the
opposite to that which makes them angry, as when they are amus-
ing themselves or laughing or feasting; when they are feeling prosperous or successful or satisfied; when, in fine, they are enjoying
freedom from pain, or inoffensive pleasure, or justifiable hope. 5
Also when time has passed and their anger is no longer fresh, for
time puts an end to anger. And vengeance previously taken on
one person puts an end to even greater anger felt against another
person. Hence Philocrates, being asked by some one, at a time
when the public was angry with him, 'Why don't you defend yourself?' did right to reply, 'The time is not yet.' 'Why, when *is* the
time?' 'When I see some one else calumniated.' For men become 10
calm when they have spent their anger on somebody else. This
happened in the case of Ergophilus: though the people were more
irritated against him than against Callisthenes, they acquitted him
because they had condemned Callisthenes to death the day before. Again, men become calm if they have convicted the offender; or if he has already suffered worse things than they in their 15
anger would have themselves inflicted upon him; for they feel as

if they were already avenged. Or if they feel that they themselves
are in the wrong and are suffering justly (for anger is not excited
by what is just), since men no longer think then that they are suffering without justification; and anger, as we have seen, means
this. Hence we ought always to inflict a preliminary punishment
20   in words: if that is done, even slaves are less aggrieved by the actual punishment. We also feel calm if we think that the offender
will not see that he is punished on our account and because of the
way he has treated us. For anger has to do with individuals. This
is plain from the definition. Hence the poet has well written:

> Say that it was Odysseus, sacker of cities,

implying that Odysseus would not have considered himself
avenged unless the Cyclops perceived both by whom and for what
he had been blinded. Consequently we do not get angry with any
25   one who cannot be aware of our anger, and in particular we cease
to be angry with people once they are dead, for we feel that the
worst has been done to them, and that they will neither feel pain
nor anything else that we in our anger aim at making them feel.
And therefore the poet has well made Apollo say, in order to put a
stop to the anger of Achilles against the dead Hector,

> For behold in his fury he doeth despite to the senseless clay.

30   It is now plain that when you wish to calm others you must draw
upon these lines of argument; you must put your hearers into the
corresponding frame of mind, and represent those with whom
they are angry as formidable, or as worthy of reverence, or as benefactors, or as involuntary agents, or as much distressed at what they
have done.

Chapter 4

Let us now turn to Friendship and Enmity, and ask towards whom
35   these feelings are entertained, and why. We will begin by defining
friendship and friendly feeling. We may describe friendly feeling
towards any one as wishing for him what you believe to be good
1381ᵃ things, not for your own sake but for his, and being inclined, so far
as you can, to bring these things about. A friend is one who feels
thus and excites these feelings in return: those who think they feel
thus towards each other think themselves friends. This being assumed, it follows that your friend is the sort of man who shares
5   your pleasure in what is good and your pain in what is unpleasant,

for your sake and for no other reason. This pleasure and pain of
his will be the token of his good wishes for you, since we all feel
glad at getting what we wish for, and pained at getting what we do
not. Those, then, are friends to whom the same things are good
and evil; and those who are, moreover, friendly or unfriendly to
the same people; for in that case they must have the same wishes,   10
and thus by wishing for each other what they wish for themselves,
they show themselves each other's friends. Again, we feel friendly
to those who have treated us well, either ourselves or those we care
for, whether on a large scale, or readily, or at some particular crisis; provided it was for our own sake. And also to those who we
think *wish* to treat us well. And also to our friends' friends, and to   15
those who like, or are liked by, those whom we like ourselves. And
also to those who are enemies to those whose enemies we are, and
dislike, or are disliked by, those whom we dislike. For all such persons think the things good which we think good, so that they wish
what is good for us; and this, as we saw, is what friends must do.
And also to those who are willing to treat us well where money or   20
our personal safety is concerned: and therefore we value those
who are liberal, brave, or just. The just we consider to be those
who do not live on others; which means those who work for their
living, especially farmers and others who work with their own
hands. We also like temperate men, because they are not unjust to   25
others; and, for the same reason, those who mind their own business. And also those whose friends we wish to be, if it is plain that
they wish to be our friends: such are the morally good, and those
well thought of by every one, by the best men, or by those whom
we admire or who admire us. And also those with whom it is pleasant to live and spend our days: such are the good-tempered, and   30
those who are not too ready to show us our mistakes, and those
who are not cantankerous or quarrelsome—such people are always wanting to fight us, and those who fight us we feel wish for
the opposite of what we wish for ourselves—and those who have
the tact to make and take a joke; here both parties have the same
object in view, when they can stand being made fun of as well as   35
do it prettily themselves. And we also feel friendly towards those
who praise such good qualities as we possess, and especially if they
praise the good qualities that we are not too sure we *do* possess.   1381^b
And towards those who are cleanly in their person, their dress, and
all their way of life. And towards those who do not reproach us
with what we have done amiss to them or they have done to help
us, for both actions show a tendency to criticize us. And towards
those who do not nurse grudges or store up grievances, but are   5

always ready to make friends again; for we take it that they will behave to us just as we find them behaving to every one else. And
towards those who are not evil speakers and who are aware of neither their neighbours' bad points nor our own, but of our good
ones only, as a good man always will be. And towards those who
do not try to thwart us when we are angry or in earnest, which
10   would mean being ready to fight us. And towards those who have
some serious feeling towards us, such as admiration for us, or belief in our goodness, or pleasure in our company; especially if they
feel like this about qualities in us for which we especially wish to
be admired, esteemed, or liked. And towards those who are like
15   ourselves in character and occupation, provided they do not get in
our way or gain their living from the same source as we do—for
then it will be a case of 'potter against potter':

   Potter to potter and builder to builder begrudge their reward.

And those who desire the same things as we desire, if it is possible
for us both to share them together; otherwise the same trouble
arises here too. And towards those with whom we are on such
20   terms that, while we respect their opinions, we need not blush before them for doing what is conventionally wrong: as well as towards those before whom we should be ashamed to do anything
really wrong. Again, our rivals, and those whom we should like to
envy us—though without ill-feeling—either we like these people
or at least we wish them to like us. And we feel friendly towards
those whom we help to secure good for themselves, provided we
25   are not likely to suffer heavily by it ourselves. And those who feel
as friendly to us when we are not with them as when we are—
which is why all men feel friendly towards those who are faithful
to their dead friends. And, speaking generally, towards those who
are really fond of their friends and do not desert them in trouble;
of all good men, we feel most friendly to those who show their
goodness as friends. Also towards those who are honest with us, including those who will tell us of their own weak points: it has just
30   been said that with our friends we are not ashamed of what is conventionally wrong, and if we do have this feeling, we do not love
them; if therefore we do not have it, it looks as if we *did* love them.
We also like those with whom we do not feel frightened or
uncomfortable—nobody can like a man of whom he feels frightened. Friendship has various forms—comradeship, intimacy, kinship, and so on.
35   Things that cause friendship are: doing kindnesses; doing them
unasked; and not proclaiming the fact when they are done, which

shows that they were done for our own sake and not for some other reason.

Enmity and Hatred should clearly be studied by reference to 1382ᵃ their opposites. Enmity may be produced by anger or spite or calumny. Now whereas anger arises from offences against oneself, enmity may arise even without that; we may hate people merely because of what we take to be their character. Anger is always concerned with individuals—a Callias or a Socrates—whereas hatred   5 is directed also against classes: we all hate any thief and any informer. Moreover, anger can be cured by time; but hatred cannot. The one aims at giving pain to its object, the other at doing him harm; the angry man wants his victims to feel; the hater does not mind whether they feel or not. All painful things are felt; but the   10 greatest evils, injustice and folly, are the least felt, since their presence causes no pain. And anger is accompanied by pain, hatred is not; the angry man feels pain, but the hater does not. Much may happen to make the angry man pity those who offend him, but the hater under no circumstances wishes to pity a man whom he has once hated: for the one would have the offenders suffer for what   15 they have done; the other would have them cease to exist.

It is plain from all this that we can prove people to be friends or enemies; if they are not, we can make them out to be so; if they claim to be so, we can refute their claim; and if it is disputed whether an action was due to anger or to hatred, we can attribute it to whichever of these we prefer.

Chapter 5

To turn next to Fear, what follows will show things and persons of which, and the states of mind in which, we feel afraid. Fear may   20 be defined as a pain or disturbance due to a mental picture of some destructive or painful evil in the future. Of destructive or painful evils only; for there are some evils, e.g. wickedness or stupidity, the prospect of which does not frighten us: I mean only such as amount to great pains or losses. And even these only if they appear not remote but so near as to be imminent: we do not fear   25 things that are a very long way off: for instance, we all know we shall die, but we are not troubled thereby, because death is not close at hand. From this definition it will follow that fear is caused by whatever we feel has great power of destroying us, or of harming us in ways that tend to cause us great pain. Hence the very   30 indications of such things are terrible, making us feel that the

terrible thing itself is close at hand; the approach of what is terrible is just what we mean by 'danger'. Such indications are the enmity and anger of people who have power to do something to us;
for it is plain that they have the will to do it, and so they are on the
35   point of doing it. Also injustice in possession of power; for it is the
unjust man's will to do evil that makes him unjust. Also outraged
1382ᵇ virtue in possession of power; for it is plain that, when outraged, it
always has the will to retaliate, and now it has the power to do so.
Also fear felt by those who have the power to do something to us,
since such persons are sure to be ready to do it. And since most
5   men tend to be bad—slaves to greed, and cowards in danger—it
is, as a rule, a terrible thing to be at another man's mercy; and
therefore, if we have done anything horrible, those in the secret
terrify us with the thought that they may betray or desert us. And
those who can do us wrong are terrible to us when we are liable to
be wronged; for as a rule men do wrong to others whenever they
10 have the power to do it. And those who have been wronged, or believe themselves to be wronged, are terrible; for they are always
looking out for their opportunity. Also those who have done people wrong, if they possess power, since they stand in fear of retaliation: we have already said that wickedness possessing power is
terrible. Again, our rivals for a thing cause us fear when we cannot
both have it at once; for we are always at war with such men. We
15 also fear those who are to be feared by stronger people than ourselves: if they can hurt those stronger people, still more can they
hurt us; and, for the same reason, we fear those whom those
stronger people are actually afraid of. Also those who have destroyed people stronger than we are. Also those who are attacking
people weaker than we are: either they are already formidable, or
they will be so when they have thus grown stronger. Of those we
20 have wronged, and of our enemies or rivals, it is not the passionate and outspoken whom we have to fear, but the quiet, dissem-
bling, unscrupulous; since we never know when they are upon us,
we can never be sure they are at a safe distance. All terrible things
are more terrible if they give us no chance of retrieving a blun-
der—either no chance at all, or only one that depends on our en-
25 emies and not ourselves. Those things are also worse which we
cannot, or cannot easily, help. Speaking generally, anything
causes us to feel fear that when it happens to, or threatens, others
causes us to feel pity.

The above are, roughly, the chief things that are terrible and are
feared. Let us now describe the conditions under which we ourselves feel fear. If fear is associated with the expectation that some-

thing destructive will happen to us, plainly nobody will be afraid   30
who believes nothing can happen to him; we shall not fear things
that we believe cannot happen to us, nor people who we believe
cannot inflict them upon us; nor shall we be afraid at times when
we think ourselves safe from them. It follows therefore that fear is
felt by those who believe something to be likely to happen to
them, at the hands of particular persons, in a particular form, and   35
at a particular time. People do not believe this when they are, or 1383ᵃ
think they a are, in the midst of great prosperity, and are in consequence insolent, contemptuous, and reckless—the kind of character produced by wealth, physical strength, abundance of friends,
power: nor yet when they feel they have experienced every kind of
horror already and have grown callous about the future, like men
who are being flogged and are already nearly dead—if they are to   5
feel the anguish of uncertainty, there must be some faint expectation of escape. This appears from the fact that fear sets us thinking
what can be done, which of course nobody does when things are
hopeless. Consequently, when it is advisable that the audience
should be frightened, the orator must make them feel that they
really are in danger of something, pointing out that it has happened to others who were stronger than they are, and is happen-   10
ing, or has happened, to people like themselves, at the hands of
unexpected people, in an unexpected form, and at an unexpected
time.

Having now seen the nature of fear, and of the things that cause
it, and the various states of mind in which it is felt, we can also see
what Confidence is, about what things we feel it, and under what   15
conditions. It is the opposite of fear, and what causes it is the opposite of what causes fear; it is, therefore, the expectation associated with a mental picture of the nearness of what keeps us safe
and the absence or remoteness of what is terrible: it may be due
either to the near presence of what inspires confidence or to the
absence of what causes alarm. We feel it if we can take steps—
many, or important, or both—to cure or prevent trouble; if we   20
have neither wronged others nor been wronged by them; if we
have either no rivals at all or no strong ones; if our rivals who are
strong are our friends or have treated us well or been treated well
by us; or if those whose interest is the same as ours are the more
numerous party, or the stronger, or both.

As for our own state of mind, we feel confidence if we believe   25
we have often succeeded and never suffered reverses, or have
often met danger and escaped it safely. For there are two reasons
why human beings face danger calmly: they may have no experi-

30   ence of it, or they may have means to deal with it: thus when in
      danger at sea people may feel confident about what will happen
      either because they have no experience of bad weather, or be-
      cause their experience gives them the means of dealing with it.
      We also feel confident whenever there is nothing to terrify other
      people like ourselves, or people weaker than ourselves, or people
      than whom we believe ourselves to be stronger—and we believe
35   this if we have conquered them, or conquered others who are as
      strong as they are, or stronger. Also if we believe ourselves superior
      to our rivals in the number and importance of the advantages that
1383ᵇ make men formidable—wealth, physical strength, strong bodies of
      supporters, extensive territory, and the possession of all, or the
      most important, appliances of war. Also if we have wronged no
      one, or not many, or not those of whom we are afraid; and gener-
5   ally, if our relations with the gods are satisfactory, as will be shown
      especially by signs and oracles. The fact is that anger makes us
      confident—that anger is excited by our knowledge that we are not
      the wrongers but the wronged, and that the divine power is always
      supposed to be on the side of the wronged. Also when, at the out-
      set of an enterprise, we believe that we cannot and shall not fail,
10   or that we shall succeed completely.—So much for the causes of
      fear and confidence.

                              Chapter 6

      We now turn to Shame and Shamelessness; what follows will ex-
      plain the things that cause these feelings, and the persons before
      whom, and the states of mind under which, they are felt. Shame
      may be defined as pain or disturbance in regard to bad things,
15   whether present, past, or future, which seem likely to involve us in
      discredit; and shamelessness as contempt or indifference in regard
      to these same bad things. If this definition be granted, it follows
      that we feel shame at such bad things as we think are disgraceful
      to ourselves or to those we care for. These evils are, in the first
20   place, those due to moral badness. Such are throwing away one's
      shield or taking to flight; for these bad things are due to cowardice.
      Also, withholding a deposit or otherwise wronging people about
      money; for these acts are due to injustice. Also, having carnal in-
      tercourse with forbidden persons, at wrong times, or in wrong
      places; for these things are due to licentiousness. Also, making
      profit in petty or disgraceful ways, or out of helpless persons, e.g.
25   the poor, or the dead—whence the proverb 'He would pick a

corpse's pocket'; for all this is due to low greed and meanness.
Also, in money matters, giving less help than you might, or none
at all, or accepting help from those worse off than yourself; so also
borrowing when it will seem like begging; begging when it will
seem like asking the return of a favour; asking such a return when
it will seem like begging; praising a man *in order that* it may seem
like begging; and going on begging in spite of failure: all such ac-   30
tions are tokens of meanness. Also, praising people to their face,
and praising extravagantly a man's good points and glozing over
his weaknesses, and showing extravagant sympathy with his grief
when you are in his presence, and all that sort of thing; all this   35
shows the disposition of a flatterer. Also, refusing to endure hard-
ships that are endured by people who are older, more delicately   1384ᵃ
brought up, of higher rank, or generally less capable of endurance
than ourselves: for all this shows effeminacy. Also, accepting benefits, especially accepting them often, from another man, and
then abusing him for conferring them: all this shows a mean, ig-
noble disposition. Also, talking incessantly about yourself, making
loud professions, and appropriating the merits of others; for this is   5
due to boastfulness. The same is true of the actions due to any of
the other forms of badness of moral character, of the tokens of
such badness, &c.: they are all disgraceful and shameless. Another
sort of bad thing at which we feel shame is, lacking a share in the
honourable things shared by every one else, or by all or nearly all
who are like ourselves. By 'those like ourselves' I mean those of   10
our own race or country or age or family, and generally those who
are on our own level. Once we are on a level with others, it is a
disgrace to be, say, less well educated than they are; and so with
other advantages: all the more so, in each case, if it is seen to be
our own fault: wherever we are ourselves to blame for our present,   15
past, or future circumstances, it follows at once that this is to a
greater extent due to our moral badness. We are moreover
ashamed of having done to us, having had done, or being about to
have done to us acts that involve us in dishonour and reproach; as
when we surrender our persons, or lend ourselves to vile deeds,
e.g. when we submit to outrage. And acts of yielding to the lust of
others are shameful whether willing or unwilling (yielding to   20
force being an instance of unwillingness), since unresisting sub-
mission to them is due to unmanliness or cowardice.

These things, and others like them, are what cause the feeling
of shame. Now since shame is a mental picture of disgrace, in
which we shrink from the disgrace itself and not from its consequences, and we only care what opinion is held of us because of   25

the people who form that opinion, it follows that the people before whom we feel shame are those whose opinion of us matters to us. Such persons are: those who admire us, those whom we admire, those by whom we wish to be admired, those with whom we are competing, and those whose opinion of us we respect. We admire those, and wish those to admire us, who possess any good thing

30 that is highly esteemed; or from whom we are very anxious to get something that they are able to give us—as a lover feels. We compete with our equals. We respect, as true, the views of sensible people, such as our elders and those who have been well educated. And we feel more shame about a thing if it is done openly, before all men's eyes. Hence the proverb, 'shame dwells in the eyes'. For this reason we feel most shame before those who will always be with us and those who notice what we do, since in both cases eyes

1384ᵇ are upon us. We also feel it before those not open to the same imputation as ourselves: for it is plain that their opinions about it are the opposite of ours. Also before those who are hard on any one whose conduct they think wrong; for what a man does himself, he is said not to resent when his neighbours do it: so that of course he

5 does resent their doing what he does not do himself. And before those who are likely to tell everybody about you; not telling others is as good as not believing you wrong. People are likely to tell others about you if you have wronged them, since they are on the look out to harm you; or if they speak evil of everybody, for those who attack the innocent will be still more ready to attack the guilty. And before those whose main occupation is with their

10 neighbours' failings—people like satirists and writers of comedy; these are really a kind of evil-speakers and tell-tales. And before those who have never yet known us come to grief, since their attitude to us has amounted to admiration so far: that is why we feel ashamed to refuse those a favour who ask one for the first time— we have not as yet lost credit with them. Such are those who are just beginning to wish to be our friends; for they have seen our

15 best side only (hence the appropriateness of Euripides' reply to the Syracusans): and such also are those among our old acquaintances who know nothing to our discredit. And we are ashamed not merely of the actual shameful conduct mentioned, but also of the evidences of it: not merely, for example, of actual sexual intercourse, but also of its evidences; and not merely of disgraceful acts

20 but also of disgraceful talk. Similarly we feel shame not merely in presence of the persons mentioned but also of those who will tell them what we have done, such as their servants or friends. And, generally, we feel no shame before those upon whose opinions we

quite look down as untrustworthy (no one feels shame before
small children or animals); nor are we ashamed of the same things   25
before intimates as before strangers, but before the former of what
seem genuine faults, before the latter of what seem conventional
ones.

The conditions under which we shall feel shame are these: first,
having people related to us like those before whom, as has been
said, we feel shame. These are, as was stated, persons whom we
admire, or who admire us, or by whom we wish to be admired, or   30
from whom we desire some service that we shall not obtain if we
forfeit their good opinion. These persons may be actually looking
on (as Cydias represented them in his speech on land assignments
in Samos, when he told the Athenians to imagine the Greeks to
be standing all around them, actually seeing the way they voted
and not merely going to hear about it afterwards): or again they   35
may be near at hand, or may be likely to find out about what we
do. This is why in misfortune we do not wish to be seen by those
who once wished themselves like us; for such a feeling implies admiration. And men feel shame when they have acts or exploits to
their credit on which they are bringing dishonour, whether these   1385ª
are their own, or those of their ancestors, or those of other persons
with whom they have some close connexion. Generally, we feel
shame before those for whose own misconduct we should also feel
it—those already mentioned; those who take us as their models;
those whose teachers or advisers we have been; or other people, it   5
may be, like ourselves, whose rivals we are. For there are many
things that shame before such people makes us do or leave un-
done. And we feel more shame when we are likely to be continually seen by, and go about under the eyes of, those who know of
our disgrace. Hence, when Antiphon the poet was to be cudgelled
to death by order of Dionysius, and saw those who were to perish   10
with him covering their faces as they went through the gates, he
said, 'Why do you cover your faces? Is it lest some of these specta-
tors should see you *to-morrow?*'

So much for Shame; to understand Shamelessness, we need
only consider the converse cases, and plainly we shall have all we   15
need.

Chapter 7

To take Kindness next: the definition of it will show us towards
whom it is felt, why, and in what frames of mind. Kindness—

under the influence of which a man is said to 'be kind'—may
be defined as helpfulness towards some one in need, not in return for anything, nor for the advantage of the helper himself,
20 but for that of the person helped. Kindness is great if shown to
one who is in great need, or who needs what is important and
hard to get, or who needs it at an important and difficult crisis;
or if the helper is the only, the first, or the chief person to give
the help. Natural cravings constitute such needs; and in particular cravings, accompanied by pain, for what is not being attained. The appetites are cravings of this kind: sexual desire,
25 for instance, and those which arise during bodily injuries and
in dangers; for appetite is active both in danger and in pain.
Hence those who stand by us in poverty or in banishment, even
if they do not help us much, are yet really kind to us, because
our need is great and the occasion pressing; for instance, the
man who gave the mat in the Lyceum. The helpfulness must
therefore meet, preferably, just this kind of need; and failing
just this kind, some other kind as great or greater. We now see
30 to whom, why, and under what conditions kindness is shown;
and these facts must form the basis of our arguments. We must
show that the persons helped are, or have been, in such pain
and need as has been described, and that their helpers gave, or
35 are giving, the kind of help described, in the kind of need described. We can also see how to eliminate the idea of kindness
1385ᵇ and make our opponents appear unkind: we may maintain that
they are being or have been helpful simply to promote their
own interest—this, as has been stated, is not kindness: or that
their action was accidental, or was forced upon them; or that
they were not doing a favour, but merely returning one,
whether they know this or not—in either case the action *is* a
mere return, and is therefore not a kindness even if the doer
5 does *not* know how the case stands. In considering this subject
we must look at all the 'categories': an act may be an act of
kindness because (1) it is a particular thing, (2) it has a particular magnitude or (3) quality, or (4) is done at a particular time
or (5) place. As evidence of the want of kindness, we may point
out that a smaller service had been refused to the man in need;
or that the same service, or an equal or greater one, has been
given to his enemies; these facts show that the service in question was not done for the sake of the person helped. Or we may
10 point out that the thing desired was worthless and that the
helper knew it: no one will admit that he is in need of what is
worthless.

Chapter 8

So much for Kindness and Unkindness. Let us now consider Pity, asking ourselves what things excite pity, and for what persons, and in what states of our mind pity is felt. Pity may be defined as a feeling of pain caused by the sight of some evil, destructive or painful, which befalls one who does not deserve it, and which we might expect to befall ourselves or some friends of ours, and moreover to befall us soon. In order to feel pity, we must obviously be capable of supposing that some evil may happen to us or some friends of ours, and moreover some such evil as is stated in our definition or is more or less of that kind. It is therefore not felt by those completely ruined, who suppose that no further evil can befall them, since the worst has befallen them already; nor by those who imagine themselves immensely fortunate—their feeling is rather presumptuous insolence, for when they think they possess all the good things of life, it is clear that the impossibility of evil befalling them will be included, this being one of the good things in question. Those who think evil *may* befall them are such as have already had it befall them and have safely escaped from it; elderly men, owing to their good sense and their experience; weak men, especially men inclined to cowardice; and also educated people, since these can take long views. Also those who have parents living, or children, or wives; for these are our own, and the evils mentioned above may easily befall them. And those who are neither moved by any courageous emotion such as anger or confidence (these emotions take no account of the future), nor by a disposition to presumptuous insolence (insolent men, too, take no account of the possibility that something evil will happen to them), nor yet by great fear (panic-stricken people do not feel pity, because they are taken up with what is happening to themselves); only those feel pity who are between these two extremes. In order to feel pity we must also believe in the goodness of at least some people; if you think nobody good, you will believe that everybody deserves evil fortune. And, generally, we feel pity whenever we are in the condition of remembering that similar misfortunes have happened to us or ours, or expecting them to happen in future.

So much for the mental conditions under which we feel pity. What we pity is stated clearly in the definition. All unpleasant and painful things excite pity if they tend to destroy pain and annihilate; and all such evils as are due to chance, if they are serious. The painful and destructive evils are: death in its various

forms, bodily injuries and afflictions, old age, diseases, lack of
food. The evils due to chance are: friendlessness, scarcity of
10   friends (it is a pitiful thing to be torn away from friends and companions), deformity, weakness, mutilation; evil coming from a
source from which good ought to have come; and the frequent
repetition of such misfortunes. Also the coming of good when the
worst has happened: e.g. the arrival of the Great King's gifts for
15   Diopeithes after his death. Also that either no good should have
befallen a man at all, or that he should not be able to enjoy it
when it has.

The grounds, then, on which we feel pity are these or like
these. The people we pity are: those whom we know, if only
they are not very closely related to us—in that case we feel
about them as if we were in danger ourselves. For this reason
20   Amasis did not weep, they say, at the sight of his son being led
to death, but did weep when he saw his friend begging: the latter sight was pitiful, the former terrible, and the terrible is different from the pitiful; it tends to cast out pity, and often helps
to produce the opposite of pity. Again, we feel pity when the
danger is near ourselves. Also we pity those who are like us in
25   age, character, disposition, social standing, or birth; for in all
these cases it appears more likely that the same misfortune may
befall us also. Here too we have to remember the general principle that what we fear for ourselves excites our pity when it
happens to others. Further, since it is when the sufferings of
others are close to us that they excite our pity (we cannot remember what disasters happened a hundred centuries ago, nor
look forward to what will happen a hundred centuries hereafter,
30   and therefore feel little pity, if any, for such things): it follows
that those who heighten the effect of their words with suitable
gestures, tones, dress, and dramatic action generally, are especially successful in exciting pity: they thus put the disasters before our eyes, and make them seem close to us, just coming or
1386ᵇ just past. Anything that has just happened, or is going to happen
soon, is particularly piteous: so too therefore are the tokens and
the actions of sufferers—the garments and the like of those who
have already suffered; the words and the like of those actually
suffering—of those, for instance, who are on the point of death.
5   Most piteous of all is it when, in such times of trial, the victims
are persons of noble character: whenever they are so, our pity is
especially excited, because their innocence, as well as the setting of their misfortunes before our eyes, makes their misfortunes seem close to ourselves.

Chapter 9

Most directly opposed to pity is the feeling called Indignation. Pain at unmerited good fortune is, in one sense, opposite to pain at unmerited bad fortune, and is due to the same moral qualities. Both feelings are associated with good moral character; it is our duty both to feel sympathy and pity for unmerited distress, and to feel indignation at unmerited prosperity; for whatever is undeserved is unjust, and that is why we ascribe indignation even to the gods. It might indeed be thought that envy is similarly opposed to pity, on the ground that envy is closely akin to indignation, or even the same thing. But it is not the same. It is true that it also is a disturbing pain excited by the prosperity of others. But it is excited not by the prosperity of the undeserving but by that of people who are like us or equal with us. The two feelings have this in common, that they must be due not to some untoward thing being likely to befall ourselves, but only to what is happening to our neighbour. The feeling ceases to be envy in the one case and indignation in the other, and becomes fear, if the pain and disturbance are due to the prospect of something bad for ourselves as the result of the other man's good fortune. The feelings of pity and indignation will obviously be attended by the converse feelings of satisfaction. If you are pained by the unmerited distress of others, you will be pleased, or at least not pained, by their merited distress. Thus no good man can be pained by the punishment of parricides or murderers. These are things we are bound to rejoice at, as we must at the prosperity of the deserving; both these things are just, and both give pleasure to any honest man, since he cannot help expecting that what has happened to a man like him will happen to him too. All these feelings are associated with the same type of moral character. And their contraries are associated with the contrary type; the man who is delighted by others' misfortunes is identical with the man who envies others' prosperity. For any one who is pained by the occurrence or existence of a given thing must be pleased by that thing's non-existence or destruction. We can now see that all these feelings tend to prevent pity (though they differ among themselves, for the reasons given), so that all are equally useful for neutralizing an appeal to pity.

We will first consider Indignation—reserving the other emotions for subsequent discussion—and ask with whom, on what grounds, and in what states of mind we may be indignant. These questions are really answered by what has been said already. Indignation is pain caused by the sight of undeserved good

10 fortune. It is, then, plain to begin with that there are some forms
of good the sight of which cannot cause it. Thus a man may be
just or brave, or acquire moral goodness: but we shall not be indignant with him for that reason, any more than we shall pity him
for the contrary reason. Indignation is roused by the sight of
wealth, power, and the like—by all those things, roughly speaking,
15 which are deserved by good men and by those who possess the
goods of nature—noble birth, beauty, and so on. Again, what is
long established seems akin to what exists by nature; and therefore
we feel more indignation at those possessing a given good if they
have as a matter of fact only just got it and the prosperity it brings
with it. The newly rich give more offence than those whose wealth
20 is of long standing and inherited. The same is true of those who
have office or power, plenty of friends, a fine family, &c. We feel
the same when these advantages of theirs secure them others. For
here again, the newly rich give us more offence by obtaining office through their riches than do those whose wealth is of long
standing; and so in all other cases. The reason is that what the lat-
25 ter have is felt to be really their own, but what the others have is
not; what appears to have been always what it is is regarded as real,
and so the possessions of the newly rich do not seem to be really
their own. Further, it is not any and every man that deserves any
given kind of good; there is a certain correspondence and appropriateness in such things; thus it is appropriate for brave men, not
30 for just men, to have fine weapons, and for men of family, not for
parvenus, to make distinguished marriages. Indignation may
therefore properly be felt when any one gets what is not appropriate for him, though he may be a good man enough. It may also be
felt when any one sets himself up against his superior, especially
against his superior in some particular respect—whence the lines

Only from battle he shrank with Aias Telamon's son;
Zeus had been angered with him, had he fought with a mightier one,

1387ᵇ but also, even apart from that, when the inferior in any sense con-
tends with his superior; a musician, for instance, with a just man,
for justice is a finer thing than music.

Enough has been said to make clear the grounds on which, and
the persons against whom, Indignation is felt—they are those
mentioned, and others like them. As for the people who feel it; we
5 feel it if we do ourselves deserve the greatest possible goods and
moreover have them, for it is an injustice that those who are not
our equals should have been held to deserve as much as we have.
Or, secondly, we feel it if we are really good and honest people;

our judgement is then sound, and we loathe any kind of injustice.
Also if we are ambitious and eager to gain particular ends, especially if we are ambitious for what others are getting without de-   10
serving to get it. And, generally, if we think that we ourselves
deserve a thing and that others do not, we are disposed to be indignant with those others so far as that thing is concerned. Hence
servile, worthless, unambitious persons are not inclined to
Indignation, since there is nothing they can believe themselves to
deserve.

From all this it is plain what sort of men those are at whose misfortunes, distresses, or failures we ought to feel pleased, or at least   15
not pained: by considering the facts described we see at once what
their contraries are. If therefore our speech puts the judges in such
a frame of mind as that indicated and shows that those who claim
pity on certain definite grounds do not deserve to secure pity but
do deserve not to secure it, it will be impossible for the judges to   20
feel pity.

Chapter 10

To take Envy next: we can see on what grounds, against what persons, and in what states of mind we feel it. Envy is pain at the sight
of such good fortune as consists of the good things already mentioned; we feel it towards our equals; not with the idea of getting
something for ourselves, but because the other people have it. We
shall feel it if we have, or think we have, equals; and by 'equals' I   25
mean equals in birth, relationship, age, disposition, distinction, or
wealth. We feel envy also if we fall but a little short of having
everything; which is why people in high place and prosperity feel
it—they think every one else is taking what belongs to themselves.
Also if we are exceptionally distinguished for some particular
thing, and especially if that thing is wisdom or good fortune.   30
Ambitious men are more envious than those who are not. So also
those who profess wisdom; they are ambitious—to be thought
wise. Indeed, generally, those who aim at a reputation for anything are envious on this particular point. And small-minded men
are envious, for everything seems great to them. The good things
which excite envy have already been mentioned. The deeds or 1388ᵃ
possessions which arouse the love of reputation and honour and
the desire for fame, and the various gifts of fortune, are almost all
subject to envy; and particularly if we desire the thing ourselves,
or think we are entitled to it, or if having it puts us a little above

others, or not having it a little below them. It is clear also what
5　kind of people we envy; that was included in what has been said
already: we envy those who are near us in time, place, age, or reputation. Hence the line:

> Ay, kin can even be jealous of their kin.

Also our fellow-competitors, who are indeed the people just mentioned—we do not compete with men who lived a hundred centuries ago, or those not yet born, or the dead, or those who dwell
10　near the Pillars of Hercules, or those whom, in our opinion or that
of others, we take to be far below us or far above us. So too we
compete with those who follow the same ends as ourselves: we
compete with our rivals in sport or in love, and generally with
those who are after the same things; and it is therefore these whom
15　we are bound to envy beyond all others. Hence the saying:

> Potter against potter.

We also envy those whose possession of or success in a thing is a
reproach to us: these are our neighbours and equals; for it is clear
that it is our own fault we have missed the good thing in question;
20　this annoys us, and excites envy in us. We also envy those who
have what we ought to have, or have got what we did have once.
Hence old men envy younger men, and those who have spent
much envy those who have spent little on the same thing. And
men who have not got a thing, or not got it yet, envy those who
have got it quickly. We can also see what things and what persons
give pleasure to envious people, and in what states of mind they
25　feel it: the states of mind in which they feel pain are those under
which they will feel pleasure in the contrary things. If therefore we
ourselves with whom the decision rests are put into an envious
state of mind, and those for whom our pity, or the award of something desirable, is claimed are such as have been described, it is
obvious that they will win no pity from us.

Chapter 11

We will next consider Emulation, showing in what follows its
causes and objects, and the state of mind in which it is felt.
30　Emulation is pain caused by seeing the presence, in persons
whose nature is like our own, of good things that are highly valued
and are possible for ourselves to acquire; but it is felt not because
others have these goods, but because we have not got them our-

selves. It is therefore a good feeling felt by good persons, whereas
envy is a bad feeling felt by bad persons. Emulation makes us take
steps to secure the good things in question, envy makes us take   35
steps to stop our neighbour having them. Emulation must therefore tend to be felt by persons who believe themselves to deserve
certain good things that they have not got, it being understood that 1388ᵇ
no one aspires to things which appear impossible. It is accordingly
felt by the young and by persons of lofty disposition. Also by those
who possess such good things as are deserved by men held in honour—these are wealth, abundance of friends, public office, and
the like; on the assumption that they ought to be good men, they   5
are emulous to gain such goods because they ought, in their belief, to belong to men whose state of mind is good. Also by those
whom all others think deserving. We also feel it about anything for
which our ancestors, relatives, personal friends, race, or country
are specially honoured, looking upon that thing as really our own,
and therefore feeling that we deserve to have it. Further, since all   10
good things that are highly honoured are objects of emulation,
moral goodness in its various forms must be such an object, and
also all those good things that are useful and serviceable to others:
for men honour those who are morally good, and also those who
do them service. So with those good things our possession of
which can give enjoyment to our neighbours—wealth and beauty
rather than health. We can see, too, what persons are the objects   15
of the feeling. They are those who have these and similar things—
those already mentioned, as courage, wisdom, public office.
Holders of public office—generals, orators, and all who possess
such powers—can do many people a good turn. Also those whom
many people wish to be like; those who have many acquaintances
or friends; those whom many admire, or whom we ourselves admire; and those who have been praised and eulogized by poets or   20
prose-writers. Persons of the contrary sort are objects of contempt:
for the feeling and notion of contempt are opposite to those of emulation. Those who are such as to emulate or be emulated by others are inevitably disposed to be contemptuous of all such persons
as are subject to those bad things which are contrary to the good   25
things that are the objects of emulation: despising them for just
that reason. Hence we often despise the fortunate, when luck
comes to them without their having those good things which are
held in honour.

   This completes our discussion of the means by which the several emotions may be produced or dissipated, and upon which depend the persuasive arguments connected with the emotions.   30

Chapter 12

Let us now consider the various types of human character, in relation to the emotions and moral qualities, showing how they correspond to our various ages and fortunes. By emotions I mean anger, desire, and the like; these we have discussed already. By moral qualities I mean virtues and vices; these also have been discussed already, as well as the various things that various types of men tend to will and to do. By ages I mean youth, the prime of
35 life, and old age. By fortune I mean birth, wealth, power, and their
1389ª opposites—in fact, good fortune and ill fortune.

To begin with the Youthful type of character. Young men have strong passions, and tend to gratify them indiscriminately. Of the
5 bodily desires, it is the sexual by which they are most swayed and in which they show absence of self-control. They are changeable and fickle in their desires, which are violent while they last, but quickly over: their impulses are keen but not deep-rooted, and are like sick people's attacks of hunger and thirst. They are hot-tempered and quick-tempered, and apt to give way to their anger;
10 bad temper often gets the better of them, for owing to their love of honour they cannot bear being slighted, and are indignant if they imagine themselves unfairly treated. While they love honour, they love victory still more; for youth is eager for superiority over others, and victory is one form of this. They love both more than they love money, which indeed they love very little, not having yet
15 learnt what it means to be without it—this is the point of Pittacus' remark about Amphiaraus. They look at the good side rather than the bad, not having yet witnessed many instances of wickedness. They trust others readily, because they have not yet often been cheated. They are sanguine; nature warms their blood as though
20 with excess of wine; and besides that, they have as yet met with few disappointments. Their lives are mainly spent not in memory but in expectation; for expectation refers to the future, memory to the past, and youth has a long future before it and a short past behind it: on the first day of one's life one has nothing at all to remember, and can only look forward. They are easily cheated, owing to the
25 sanguine disposition just mentioned. Their hot tempers and hopeful dispositions make them more courageous than older men are; the hot temper prevents fear, and the hopeful disposition creates confidence; we cannot feel fear so long as we are feeling angry, and any expectation of good makes us confident. They are shy, accepting the rules of society in which they have been trained, and
30 not yet believing in any other standard of honour. They have ex-

alted notions, because they have not yet been humbled by life or
learnt its necessary limitations; moreover, their hopeful disposition makes them think themselves equal to great things—and that
means having exalted notions. They would always rather do noble
deeds than useful ones: their lives are regulated more by moral
feeling than by reasoning; and whereas reasoning leads us to
choose what is useful, moral goodness leads us to choose what is
noble. They are fonder of their friends, intimates, and compan-   35
ions than older men are, because they like spending their days in   1389ᵇ
the company of others, and have not yet come to value either their
friends or anything else by their usefulness to themselves. All their
mistakes are in the direction of doing things excessively and vehe-
mently. They disobey Chilon's precept by overdoing everything;
they love too much and hate too much, and the same thing with   5
everything else. They think they know everything, and are always
quite sure about it; this, in fact, is why they overdo everything. If
they do wrong to others, it is because they mean to insult them,
not to do them actual harm. They are ready to pity others, because
they think every one an honest man, or anyhow better than he is:
they judge their neighbour by their own harmless natures, and so
cannot think he deserves to be treated in that way. They are fond   10
of fun and therefore witty, wit being well-bred insolence.

Chapter 13

Such, then, is the character of the Young. The character of
Elderly Men—men who are past their prime—may be said to be
formed for the most part of elements that are the contrary of all
these. They have lived many years; they have often been taken in,   15
and often made mistakes; and life on the whole is a bad business.
The result is that they are sure about nothing and *under-do* everything. They 'think', but they never 'know'; and because of their
hesitation they always add a 'possibly' or a 'perhaps', putting everything this way and nothing positively. They are cynical; that is,
they tend to put the worse construction on everything. Further,   20
their experience makes them distrustful and therefore suspicious
of evil. Consequently they neither love warmly nor hate bitterly,
but following the hint of Bias they love as though they will some
day hate and hate as though they will some day love. They are
small-minded, because they have been humbled by life: their de-   25
sires are set upon nothing more exalted or unusual than what will
help them to keep alive. They are not generous, because money is

one of the things they must have, and at the same time their experience has taught them how hard it is to get and how easy to
30   lose. They are cowardly, and are always anticipating danger; unlike that of the young, who are warm-blooded, their temperament
is chilly; old age has paved the way for cowardice; fear is, in fact,
a form of chill. They love life; and all the more when their last day
has come, because the object of all desire is something we have
35   not got, and also because we desire most strongly that which we
need most urgently. They are too fond of themselves; this is one
form that small-mindedness takes. Because of this, they guide
their lives too much by considerations of what is useful and too lit-
1390ᵃ tle by what is noble—for the useful is what is good for oneself, and
the noble what is good absolutely. They are not shy, but shameless
rather; caring less for what is noble than for what is useful, they
feel contempt for what people may think of them. They lack confidence in the future; partly through experience—for most things
5   go wrong, or anyhow turn out worse than one expects; and partly
because of their cowardice. They live by memory rather than by
hope; for what is left to them of life is but little as compared with
the long past; and hope is of the future, memory of the past. This,
10   again, is the cause of their loquacity; they are continually talking
of the past, because they enjoy remembering it. Their fits of anger
are sudden but feeble. Their sensual passions have either altogether gone or have lost their vigour: consequently they do not
feel their passions much, and their actions are inspired less by
what they do feel than by the love of gain. Hence men at this time
15   of life are often supposed to have a self-controlled character; the
fact is that their passions have slackened, and they are slaves to the
love of gain. They guide their lives by reasoning more than by
moral feeling; reasoning being directed to utility and moral feeling to moral goodness. If they wrong others, they mean to injure
them, not to insult them. Old men may feel pity, as well as young
20   men, but not for the same reason. Young men feel it out of kindness; old men out of weakness, imagining that anything that befalls any one else might easily happen to them, which, as we saw,
is a thought that excites pity. Hence they are querulous, and not
disposed to jesting or laughter—the love of laughter being the very
opposite of querulousness.

Such are the characters of Young Men and Elderly Men.
25   People always think well of speeches adapted to, and reflecting,
their own character: and we can now see how to compose our
speeches so as to adapt both them and ourselves to our audiences.

Chapter 14

As for Men in their Prime, clearly we shall find that they have a
character between that of the young and that of the old, free from
the extremes of either. They have neither that excess of confi-   30
dence which amounts to rashness, nor too much timidity, but the
right amount of each. They neither trust everybody nor distrust
everybody, but judge people correctly. Their lives will be guided
not by the sole consideration either of what is noble or of what is   1390^b
useful, but by both; neither by parsimony nor by prodigality, but
by what is fit and proper. So, too, in regard to anger and desire;
they will be brave as well as temperate, and temperate as well as   5
brave; these virtues are divided between the young and the old;
the young are brave but intemperate, the old temperate but cowardly. To put it generally, all the valuable qualities that youth and
age divide between them are united in the prime of life, while all
their excesses or defects are replaced by moderation and fitness.
The body is in its prime from thirty to five-and-thirty; the mind   10
about forty-nine.

Chapter 15

So much for the types of character that distinguish youth, old age,
and the prime of life. We will now turn to those Gifts of Fortune
by which human character is affected. First let us consider Good   15
Birth. Its effect on character is to make those who have it more
ambitious; it is the way of all men who have something to start
with to add to the pile, and good birth implies ancestral distinction. The well-born man will look down even on those who are as   20
good as his own ancestors, because any far-off distinction is greater
than the same thing close to us, and better to boast about. Being
well-born, which means coming of a fine stock, must be distinguished from nobility, which means being true to the family nature—a quality not usually found in the well-born, most of whom
are poor creatures. In the generations of men as in the fruits of the   25
earth, there is a varying yield; now and then, where the stock is
good, exceptional men are produced for a while, and then deca-
dence sets in. A clever stock will degenerate towards the insane
type of character, like the descendants of Alcibiades or of the elder
Dionysius; a steady stock towards the fatuous and torpid type, like   30
the descendants of Cimon, Pericles, and Socrates.

Chapter 16

The type of character produced by Wealth lies on the surface for all to see. Wealthy men are insolent and arrogant; their possession of wealth affects their understanding; they feel as if they had every good thing that exists; wealth becomes a sort of standard of value 1391ᵃ for everything else, and therefore they imagine there is nothing it cannot buy. They are luxurious and ostentatious; luxurious, because of the luxury in which they live and the prosperity which they display; ostentatious and vulgar, because, like other people's, 5 their minds are regularly occupied with the object of their love and admiration, and also because they think that other people's idea of happiness is the same as their own. It is indeed quite natural that they should be affected thus; for if you have money, there are always plenty of people who come begging from you. Hence the saying of Simonides about wise men and rich men, in answer to Hiero's wife, who asked him whether it was better to grow rich 10 or wise. 'Why, rich,' he said; 'for I see the wise men spending their days at the rich men's doors.' Rich men also consider themselves worthy to hold public office; for they consider they already have the things that give a claim to office. In a word, the type of character produced by wealth is that of a prosperous fool. There is indeed one difference between the type of the newly-enriched and 15 those who have long been rich: the newly-enriched have all the bad qualities mentioned in an exaggerated and worse form—to be newly-enriched means, so to speak, *no education in riches*. The wrongs they do others are not meant to injure their victims, but spring from insolence or self-indulgence, e.g. those that end in assault or in adultery.

Chapter 17

20 As to Power: here too it may fairly be said that the type of character it produces is mostly obvious enough. Some elements in this type it shares with the wealthy type, others are better. Those in power are more ambitious and more manly in character than the wealthy, because they aspire to do the great deeds that their power 25 permits them to do. Responsibility makes them more serious: they have to keep paying attention to the duties their position involves. They are dignified rather than arrogant, for the respect in which they are held inspires them with dignity and therefore with moderation—dignity being a mild and becoming form of

arrogance. If they wrong others, they wrong them not on a small but on a great scale.

Good fortune in certain of its branches produces the types of character belonging to the conditions just described, since these conditions are in fact more or less the kinds of good fortune that are regarded as most important. It may be added that good fortune leads us to gain all we can in the way of family happiness and bodily advantages. It does indeed make men more supercilious and more reckless; but there is one excellent quality that goes with it— piety, and respect for the divine power, in which they believe because of events which are really the result of chance.

This account of the types of character that correspond to differences of age or fortune may end here; for to arrive at the opposite types to those described, namely, those of the poor, the unfortunate, and the powerless, we have only to ask what the opposite qualities are.

Chapter 18

The use of persuasive speech is to lead to decisions. (When we know a thing, and have decided about it, there is no further use in speaking about it.) This is so even if one is addressing a single person and urging him to do or not to do something, as when we scold a man for his conduct or try to change his views: the single person is as much your 'judge' as if he were one of many; we may say, without qualification, that any one is your judge whom you have to persuade. Nor does it matter whether we are arguing against an actual opponent or against a mere proposition; in the latter case we still have to use speech and overthrow the opposing arguments, and we attack these as we should attack an actual opponent. Our principle holds good of ceremonial speeches also; the 'onlookers' for whom such a speech is put together are treated as the judges of it. Broadly speaking, however, the only sort of person who can strictly be called a judge is the man who decides the issue in some matter of public controversy; that is, in law suits and in political debates, in both of which there are issues to be decided. In the section on political oratory an account has already been given of the types of character that mark the different constitutions.

The manner and means of investing speeches with moral character may now be regarded as fully set forth.

Each of the main divisions of oratory has, we have seen, its own

distinct purpose. With regard to each division, we have noted the
25 accepted views and propositions upon which we may base our
arguments—for political, for ceremonial, and for forensic speaking. We have further determined completely by what means
speeches may be invested with the required moral character. We
are now to proceed to discuss the arguments common to *all* oratory. All orators, besides their special lines of argument, are bound
30 to use, for instance, the topic of the Possible and Impossible; and
to try to show that a thing has happened, or will happen in future.
Again, the topic of Size is common to all oratory; all of us have to
argue that things are bigger or smaller than they seem, whether we
are making political speeches, speeches of eulogy or attack, or
1392ᵃ prosecuting or defending in the law-courts. Having analysed these
subjects, we will try to say what we can about the general principles of arguing by 'enthymeme' and 'example', by the addition of
which we may hope to complete the project with which we set
out. Of the above-mentioned general lines of argument, that concerned with Amplification is—as has been already said—most ap-
5 propriate to ceremonial speeches; that concerned with the Past, to
forensic speeches, where the required decision is always about the
past; that concerned with Possibility and the Future, to political
speeches.

Chapter 19

Let us first speak of the Possible and Impossible. It may plausibly
be argued: That if it is possible for one of a pair of contraries to be
10 or happen, then it is possible for the other: e.g. if a man can be
cured, he can also fall ill; for any two contraries are equally possible, in so far as they are contraries. That if of two similar things
one is possible, so is the other. That if the harder of two things is
possible, so is the easier. That if a thing can come into existence
in a good and beautiful form, then it can come into existence gen-
15 erally; thus a house can exist more easily than a beautiful house.
That if the beginning of a thing can occur, so can the end; for
nothing impossible occurs or begins to occur; thus the commen-
surability of the diagonal of a square with its side neither occurs
nor can begin to occur. That if the end is possible, so is the be-
20 ginning; for all things that occur have a beginning. That if that
which is posterior in essence or in order of generation can come
into being, so can that which is prior: thus if a man can come into
being, so can a boy, since the boy comes first in order of genera-

tion; and if a boy can, so can a man, for the man also is first. That
those things are possible of which the love or desire is natural; for   25
no one, as a rule, loves or desires impossibilities. That things
which are the object of any kind of science or art are possible and
exist or come into existence. That anything is possible the first step
in whose production depends on men or things which we can
compel or persuade to produce it, by our greater strength, our
control of them, or our friendship with them. That where the parts   30
are possible, the whole is possible; and where the whole is possible, the parts are usually possible. For if the slit in front, the toe-
piece, and the upper leather can be made, then shoes can be
made; and if shoes, then also the front slit and toe-piece. That if a   1392^b
whole genus is a thing that can occur, so can the species; and if
the species can occur, so can the genus: thus, if a sailing vessel can
be made, so also can a trireme; and if a trireme, then a sailing vessel also. That if one of two things whose existence depends on
each other is possible, so is the other; for instance, if 'double', then
'half', and if 'half', then 'double'. That if a thing can be produced   5
without art or preparation, it can be produced still more certainly
by the careful application of art to it. Hence Agathon has said:

> To some things we by art must needs attain,
> Others by destiny or luck we gain.

That if anything is possible to inferior, weaker, and stupider peo-   10
ple, it is more so for their opposites; thus Isocrates said that it
would be a strange thing if he could not discover a thing that
Euthynus had found out. As for Impossibility, we can clearly get
what we want by taking the contraries of the arguments stated
above.

Questions of Past Fact may be looked at in the following ways:
First, that if the less likely of two things has occurred, the more   15
likely must have occurred also. That if one thing that usually follows another has happened, then that other thing has happened;
that, for instance, if a man has forgotten a thing, he has also once
learnt it. That if a man had the power and the wish to do a thing,
he has done it; for every one does do whatever he intends to do
whenever he can do it, there being nothing to stop him. That,   20
further, he has done the thing in question either if he intended
it and nothing external prevented him; or if he had the power to
do it and was angry at the time; or if he had the power to do it
and his heart was set upon it—for people as a rule do what they
long to do, if they can; bad people through lack of self-control;
good people, because their hearts are set upon good things.   25

Again, that if a thing was 'going to happen', it has happened; if a
man was 'going to do something', he has done it, for it is likely
that the intention was carried out. That if one thing has happened which naturally happens before another or with a view to
it, the other has happened; for instance, if it has lightened, it has
also thundered; and if an action has been attempted, it has been
done. That if one thing has happened which naturally happens
after another, or with a view to which that other happens, then
that other (that which happens first, or happens with a view to
30   this thing) has also happened; thus, if it has thundered it has
lightened, and if an action has been done it has been attempted.
Of all these sequences some are inevitable and some merely
usual. The arguments for the *non*-occurrence of anything can
obviously be found by considering the opposites of those that
have been mentioned.

1393ᵃ   How questions of Future Fact should be argued is clear
from the same considerations: That a thing will be done if
there is both the power and the wish to do it; or if along with
the power to do it there is a craving for the result, or anger, or
calculation, prompting it. That the thing will be done, in
these cases, if the man is actually setting about it, or even if he
5   means to do it later—for usually what we mean to do happens
rather than what we do not mean to do. That a thing will happen if another thing which naturally happens before it has already happened; thus, if it is clouding over, it is likely to rain.
That if the means to an end have occurred, then the end is
likely to occur; thus, if there is a foundation, there will be a
house.

For arguments about the Greatness and Smallness of things, the
10   greater and the lesser, and generally great things and small, what
we have already said will show the line to take. In discussing deliberative oratory we have spoken about the relative greatness of
various goods, and about the greater and lesser in general. Since
therefore in each type of oratory the object under discussion is
some kind of good—whether it is utility, nobleness, or justice—it
is clear that every orator must obtain the materials of amplification
15   through these channels. To go further than this, and try to establish abstract laws of greatness and superiority, is to argue without
an object; in practical life, particular facts count more than gen-
eralizations.

Enough has now been said about these questions of possibility
20   and the reverse, of past or future fact, and of the relative greatness
or smallness of things.

Chapter 20

The special forms of oratorical argument having now been discussed, we have next to treat of those which are common to all kinds of oratory. These are of two main kinds, 'Example' and 'Enthymeme'; for the 'Maxim' is part of an enthymeme.

We will first treat of argument by Example, for it has the nature 25 of induction, which is the foundation of reasoning. This form of argument has two varieties; one consisting in the mention of actual past facts, the other in the invention of facts by the speaker. Of the latter, again, there are two varieties, the illustrative parallel and the fable (e.g. the fables of Aesop, or those from Libya). As an 30 instance of the mention of actual facts, take the following. The speaker may argue thus: 'We must prepare for war against the king of Persia and not let him subdue Egypt. For Darius of old did not 1393^b cross the Aegean until he had seized Egypt; but once he had seized it, he did cross. And Xerxes, again, did not attack us until he had seized Egypt; but once he had seized it, he did cross. If therefore the present king seizes Egypt, he also will cross, and therefore we must not let him.'

The illustrative parallel is the sort of argument Socrates used: e.g. 'Public officials ought not to be selected by lot. That is like using the lot to select athletes, instead of choosing those who are 5 fit for the contest; or using the lot to select a steersman from among a ship's crew, as if we ought to take the man on whom the lot falls, and not the man who knows most about it.'

Instances of the fable are that of Stesichorus about Phalaris, and that of Aesop in defence of the popular leader. When the people of Himera had made Phalaris military dictator, and were going to 10 give him a bodyguard, Stesichorus wound up a long talk by telling them the fable of the horse who had a field all to himself. Presently there came a stag and began to spoil his pasturage. The horse, wishing to revenge himself on the stag, asked a man if he 15 could help him to do so. The man said, 'Yes, if you will let me bridle you and get on to your back with javelins in my hand'. The horse agreed, and the man mounted; but instead of getting his revenge on the stag, the horse found himself the slave of the man. 'You too', said Stesichorus, 'take care lest in your desire for re- 20 venge on your enemies, you meet the same fate as the horse. By making Phalaris military dictator, you have already let yourselves be bridled. If you let him get on to your backs by giving him a bodyguard, from that moment you will be his slaves.'

Aesop, defending before the assembly at Samos a popular

leader who was being tried for his life, told this story: A fox, in
25   crossing a river, was swept into a hole in the rocks; and, not being
able to get out, suffered miseries for a long time through the
swarms of fleas that fastened on her. A hedgehog, while roaming
around, noticed the fox; and feeling sorry for her asked if he might
remove the fleas. But the fox declined the offer; and when the
hedgehog asked why, she replied, 'These fleas are by this time full
30   of me and not sucking much blood; if you take them away, others
will come with fresh appetites and drink up all the blood I have
left.' 'So, men of Samos', said Aesop, 'my client will do you no further harm; he is wealthy already. But if you put him to death, oth-
1394ª ers will come along who are not rich, and their peculations will
empty your treasury completely.'

Fables are suitable for addresses to popular assemblies; and they
have one advantage—they are comparatively easy to invent,
whereas it is hard to find parallels among actual past events. You
5   will in fact frame them just as you frame illustrative parallels: all
you require is the power of thinking out your analogy, a power developed by intellectual training. But while it is easier to supply
parallels by inventing fables, it is more valuable for the political
speaker to supply them by quoting what has actually happened,
since in most respects the future will be like what the past has
been.

Where we are unable to argue by Enthymeme, we must try to
10   demonstrate our point by this method of Example, and to convince our hearers thereby. If we *can* argue by Enthymeme, we
should use our Examples as subsequent supplementary evidence.
They should not precede the Enthymemes: that will give the argument an inductive air, which only rarely suits the conditions of
speech-making. If they follow the enthymemes, they have the effect of witnesses giving evidence, and this always tells. For the
15   same reason, if you put your examples first you must give a large
number of them; if you put them last, a single one is sufficient;
even a single witness will serve if he is a good one. It has now been
stated how many varieties of argument by Example there are, and
how and when they are to be employed.

Chapter 21

We now turn to the use of Maxims, in order to see upon what sub-
20   jects and occasions, and for what kind of speaker, they will appro-
priately form part of a speech. This will appear most clearly when

we have defined a maxim. It is a statement; not a particular fact, such as the character of Iphicrates, but of a general kind; nor is it about any and every subject—e.g. 'straight is the contrary of curved' is not a maxim—but only about questions of practical conduct, courses of conduct to be chosen or avoided. Now an Enthymeme is a syllogism dealing with such practical subjects. It is therefore roughly true that the premisses or conclusions of Enthymemes, considered apart from the rest of the argument, are Maxims: e.g.

> Never should any man whose wits are sound
> Have his sons taught more wisdom than their fellows.

Here we have a Maxim; add the reason or explanation, and the whole thing is an Enthymeme; thus—

> It makes them idle; and therewith they earn
> Ill-will and jealousy throughout the city.

Again,   1394ᵇ

> There is no man in all things prosperous,

and

> There is no man among us all is free,

are maxims; but the latter, taken with what follows it, is an Enthymeme—

> For all are slaves of money or of chance.

From this definition of a maxim it follows that there are four kinds of maxims. In the first place, the maxim may or may not have a supplement. Proof is needed where the statement is paradoxical or disputable; no supplement is wanted where the statement contains nothing paradoxical, either because the view expressed is already a known truth, e.g.

> Chiefest of blessings is health for a man, as it seemeth to me,

this being the general opinion: or because, as soon as the view is stated, it is clear at a glance, e.g.

> No love is true save that which loves for ever.

Of the Maxims that do have a supplement attached, some are part of an Enthymeme, e.g.

> Never should any man whose wits are sound, &c.

Others have the essential character of Enthymemes, but are not
stated as parts of Enthymemes; these latter are reckoned the best;
20   they are those in which the reason for the view expressed is simply
implied, e.g.

> O mortal man, nurse not immortal wrath.

To say 'it is not right to nurse immortal wrath' is a maxim; the
added words 'O mortal man' give the reason. Similarly, with the
words

> Mortal creatures ought to cherish mortal, not immortal thoughts.

25   What has been said has shown us how many kinds of Maxim
there are, and to what subjects the various kinds are appropriate.
They must not be given without supplement if they express disputed or paradoxical views: we must, in that case, either put the
supplement first and make a maxim of the conclusion, e.g. you
30   might say, 'For my part, since both unpopularity and idleness are
undesirable, I hold that it is better not to be educated'; or you may
say this first, and then add the previous clause. Where a statement,
without being paradoxical, is not obviously true, the reason should
be added as concisely as possible. In such cases both laconic and
1395ᵃ enigmatic sayings are suitable: thus one might say what
Stesichorus said to the Locrians, 'Insolence is better avoided, lest
the cicalas chirp on the ground'.

    The use of Maxims is appropriate only to elderly men, and in
handling subjects in which the speaker is experienced. For a
young man to use them is—like telling stories—unbecoming; to
use them in handling things in which one has no experience is
5   silly and ill-bred: a fact sufficiently proved by the special fondness
of country fellows for striking out maxims, and their readiness to
air them.

    To declare a thing to be universally true when it is not is most
appropriate when working up feelings of horror and indignation
in our hearers; especially by way of preface, or after the facts have
10   been proved. Even hackneyed and commonplace maxims are to
be used, if they suit one's purpose: just because they are commonplace, every one seems to agree with them, and therefore they
are taken for truth. Thus, any one who is calling on his men to risk
an engagement without obtaining favourable omens may quote

> One omen of all is best, that we fight for our fatherland.

Or, if he is calling on them to attack a stronger force—

> The War-God showeth no favour.   15

Or, if he is urging people to destroy the innocent children of their enemies—

> Fool, who slayeth the father and leaveth his sons to avenge him.

Some proverbs are also maxims, e.g. the proverb 'An Attic neighbour'. You are not to avoid uttering maxims that contradict such sayings as have become public property (I mean such sayings as 'know thyself' and 'nothing in excess'), if doing so will raise your   20
hearers' opinion of your character, or convey an effect of strong emotion—e.g. an angry speaker might well say, 'It is not true that we ought to know ourselves: anyhow, if this man had known himself, he would never have thought himself fit for an army command.' It will raise people's opinion of our character to say, for instance, 'We ought not to follow the saying that bids us treat our   25
friends as future enemies: much better to treat our enemies as future friends.' The moral purpose should be implied partly by the very wording of our maxim. Failing this, we should add our reason: e.g. having said 'We should treat our friends, not as the saying advises, but as if they were going to be our friends always', we should add 'for the other behaviour is that of a traitor': or we might   30
put it, 'I disapprove of that saying. A true friend will treat his friend as if he were going to be his friend for ever'; and again, 'Nor do I approve of the saying "nothing in excess": we are bound to hate bad men excessively.'

One great advantage of Maxims to a speaker is due to the want   1395^b
of intelligence in his hearers, who love to hear him succeed in expressing as a universal truth the opinions which they hold themselves about particular cases. I will explain what I mean by this, indicating at the same time how we are to hunt down the maxims required. The maxim, as has been already said, is a general state-   5
ment and people love to hear stated in general terms what they already believe in some particular connexion: e.g. if a man happens to have bad neighbours or bad children, he will agree with any one who tells him, 'Nothing is more annoying than having neighbours', or, 'Nothing is more foolish than to be the parent of children.' The orator has therefore to guess the subjects on which his   10
hearers really hold views already, and what those views are, and then must express, as general truths, these same views on these same subjects. This is one advantage of using maxims. There is another which is more important—it invests a speech with moral character. There is moral character in every speech in which the

moral purpose is conspicuous: and maxims always produce this ef-
15   fect, because the utterance of them amounts to a general declara-
tion of moral principles: so that, if the maxims are sound, they
display the speaker as a man of sound moral character. So much
for the Maxim—its nature, varieties, proper use, and advantages.

Chapter 22

20   We now come to the Enthymemes, and will begin the subject
with some general consideration of the proper way of looking for
them, and then proceed to what is a distinct question, the lines of
argument to be embodied in them. It has already been pointed out
that the Enthymeme is a syllogism, and in what sense it is so. We
have also noted the differences between it and the syllogism of dialectic. Thus we must not carry its reasoning too far back, or the
25   length of our argument will cause obscurity: nor must we put in
all the steps that lead to our conclusion, or we shall waste words
in saying what is manifest. It is this simplicity that makes the uneducated more effective than the educated when addressing popular audiences—makes them, as the poets tell us, 'charm the
30   crowd's ears more finely'. Educated men lay down broad general
principles; uneducated men argue from common knowledge and
draw obvious conclusions. We must not, therefore, start from any
and every accepted opinion, but only from those we have
1396ª   defined—those accepted by our judges or by those whose authority they recognize: and there must, moreover, be no doubt in the
minds of most, if not all, of our judges that the opinions put forward really are of this sort. We should also base our arguments
upon probabilities as well as upon certainties.

The first thing we have to remember is this. Whether our argu-
5   ment concerns public affairs or some other subject, we must know
some, if not all, of the facts about the subject on which we are to
speak and argue. Otherwise we can have no materials out of
which to construct arguments. I mean, for instance, how could we
advise the Athenians whether they should go to war or not, if we
did not know their strength, whether it was naval or military or
10   both, and how great it is; what their revenues amount to; who their
friends and enemies are; what wars, too, they have waged, and
with what success; and so on? Or how could we eulogize them if
we knew nothing about the sea-fight at Salamis, or the battle of
Marathon, or what they did for the Heracleidae, or any other facts
15   like that? All eulogy is based upon the noble deeds—real or imag-

inary—that stand to the credit of those eulogized. On the same
principle, invectives are based on facts of the opposite kind: the orator looks to see what base deeds—real or imaginary—stand to the
discredit of those he is attacking, such as treachery to the cause of
Hellenic freedom, or the enslavement of their gallant allies against
the barbarians (Aegina, Potidaea, &c.), or any other misdeeds of
this kind that are recorded against them. So, too, in a court of law:
whether we are prosecuting or defending, we must pay attention
to the existing facts of the case. It makes no difference whether the
subject is the Lacedaemonians or the Athenians, a man or a god;
we must do the same thing. Suppose it to be Achilles whom we
are to advise, to praise or blame, to accuse or defend; here too we
must take the facts, real or imaginary; these must be our material,
whether we are to praise or blame him for the noble or base deeds
he has done, to accuse or defend him for his just or unjust treatment of others, or to advise him about what is or is not to his interest. The same thing applies to any subject whatever. Thus, in
handling the question whether justice is or is not a good, we must
start with the real facts about justice and goodness. We see, then,
that this is the only way in which any one ever proves anything,
whether his arguments are strictly cogent or not: not all facts can
form his basis, but only those that bear on the matter in hand: nor,
plainly, can proof be effected otherwise by means of the speech.
Consequently, as appears in the *Topics*, we must first of all have by
us a selection of arguments about questions that may arise and are
suitable for us to handle; and then we must try to think out arguments of the same type for special needs as they emerge; not
vaguely and indefinitely, but by keeping our eyes on the actual
facts of the subject we have to speak on, and gathering in as many
of them as we can that bear closely upon it: for the more actual
facts we have at our command, the more easily we prove our case;
and the more closely they bear on the subject, the more they will
seem to belong to that speech only instead of being commonplaces. By 'commonplaces' I mean, for example, eulogy of
Achilles because he is a human being or a demi-god, or because
he joined the expedition against Troy: these things are true of
many others, so that this kind of eulogy applies no better to
Achilles than to Diomede. The special facts here needed are those
that are true of Achilles alone; such facts as that he slew Hector,
the bravest of the Trojans, and Cycnus the invulnerable, who prevented all the Greeks from landing, and again that he was the
youngest man who joined the expedition, and was not bound by
oath to join it, and so on.

20   Here, then, we have our first principle of selection of Enthymemes—that which refers to the lines of argument selected. We
will now consider the various elementary classes of enthymemes.
(By an 'elementary class' of enthymeme I mean the same thing as
a 'line of argument'.) We will begin, as we must begin, by observ-
25   ing that there are two kinds of enthymemes. One kind proves
some affirmative or negative proposition; the other kind disproves
one. The difference between the two kinds is the same as that between syllogistic proof and disproof in dialectic. The demonstrative enthymeme is formed by the conjunction of compatible
propositions; the refutative, by the conjunction of incompatible
propositions.

We may now be said to have in our hands the lines of argument
for the various *special* subjects that it is useful or necessary to han-
30   dle, having selected the propositions suitable in various cases. We
have, in fact, already ascertained the lines of argument applicable
to enthymemes about good and evil, the noble and the base, justice and injustice, and also to those about types of character, emotions, and moral qualities. Let us now lay hold of certain facts
1397ᵃ about the whole subject, considered from a different and more
general point of view. In the course of our discussion we will take
note of the distinction between lines of proof and lines of disproof:
and also of those lines of argument used in what seem to be enthymemes, but are not, since they do not represent valid syllogisms. Having made all this clear, we will proceed to classify
5   Objections and Refutations, showing how they can be brought to
bear upon enthymemes.

Chapter 23

1. One line of positive proof is based upon consideration of the
opposite of the thing in question. Observe whether that opposite
has the opposite quality. If it has not, you refute the original propo-
10   sition; if it has, you establish it. E.g. 'Temperance is beneficial; for
licentiousness is hurtful'. Or, as in the Messenian speech, 'If war
is the cause of our present troubles, peace is what we need to put
things right again'. Or—

> For if not even evil-doers should
> Anger us if they meant not what they did,
> Then can we owe no gratitude to such
15   As were constrained to do the good they did us.

Or—

> Since in this world liars may win belief,
> Be sure of the opposite likewise—that this world
> Hears many a true word and believes it not.

2. Another line of proof is got by considering some modification
of the key-word, and arguing that what can or cannot be said of the   20
one, can or cannot be said of the other: e.g. 'just' does not always
mean 'beneficial', or 'justly' would always mean 'beneficially',
whereas it is *not* desirable to be justly put to death.

3. Another line of proof is based upon correlative ideas. If it is
true that one man *gave* noble or just treatment to another, you
argue that the other must have *received* noble or just treatment; or
that where it is right to command obedience, it must have been
right to obey the command. Thus Diomedon, the tax-farmer, said   25
of the taxes: 'If it is no disgrace for you to sell them, it is no disgrace for us to buy them'. Further, if 'well' or 'justly' is true of the
person to whom a thing is done, you argue that it is true of the
doer. But it is possible to draw a false conclusion here. It may be
just that A should be treated in a certain way, and yet *not* just that   30
he should be so treated by B. Hence you must ask yourself two distinct questions: (1) Is it right that A should be thus treated? (2) Is   1397ᵇ
it right that B should thus treat him? and apply your results properly, according as your answers are Yes or No. Sometimes in such
a case the two answers differ: you may quite easily have a position
like that in the *Alcmaeon* of Theodectes:

> And was there none to loathe thy mother's crime?

to which question Alcmaeon in reply says,

> Why, there are two things to examine here.

And when Alphesiboea asks what he means, he rejoins: 5

> They judged *her* fit to die, not *me* to slay her.

Again there is the lawsuit about Demosthenes and the men who
killed Nicanor; as they were judged to have killed him justly, it
was thought that he was killed justly. And in the case of the man
who was killed at Thebes, the judges were requested to decide   10
whether it was unjust that he should be killed, since if it was not,
it was argued that it could not have been unjust to kill him.

4. Another line of proof is the *a fortiori*. Thus it may be argued
that if even the gods are not omniscient, certainly human beings
are not. The principle here is that, if a quality does not in fact exist

where it is *more* likely to exist, it clearly does not exist where it is
15   *less* likely. Again, the argument that a man who strikes his father
also strikes his neighbours follows from the principle that, if the
less likely thing is true, the more likely thing is true also; for a man
is less likely to strike his father than to strike his neighbours. The
argument, then, may run thus. Or it may be urged that, if a thing
is not true where it is more likely, it is not true where it is less
likely; or that, if it is true where it is less likely, it is true where it is
more likely: according as we have to show that a thing *is* or is *not*
true. This argument might also be used in a case of parity, as in
the lines:

Thou hast pity for *thy* sire, who has lost his sons:
20   Hast none for Oeneus, whose brave son is dead?

And, again, 'if Theseus did no wrong, neither did Paris'; or 'if the
sons of Tyndareus did no wrong, neither did Paris'; or 'if Hector
did well to slay Patroclus, Paris did well to slay Achilles'. And 'if
other followers of an art are not bad men, neither are philosophers'. And 'if generals are not bad men because it often happens
25   that they are condemned to death, neither are sophists'. And the
remark that 'if each individual among you ought to think of his
own city's reputation, you ought all to think of the reputation of
Greece as a whole'.

    5. Another line of argument is based on considerations of time.
Thus Iphicrates, in the case against Harmodius, said, 'if before
doing the deed I had bargained that, if I did it, I should have a
statue, you would have given me one. Will you not give me one
30   now that I *have* done the deed? You must not make promises when
you are expecting a thing to be done for you, and refuse to fulfil
them when the thing has been done.' And, again, to induce the
Thebans to let Philip pass through their territory into Attica, it was
1398ª   argued that 'if he had insisted on this before he helped them
against the Phocians, they would have promised to do it. It is monstrous, therefore, that just because he threw away his advantage
then, and trusted their honour, they should not let him pass
through now'.

    6. Another line is to apply to the other speaker what he has said
against yourself. It is an excellent turn to give to a debate, as may
5   be seen in the *Teucer*. It was employed by Iphicrates in his reply
to Aristophon. 'Would *you*,' he asked, 'take a bribe to betray the
fleet?' 'No', said Aristophon; and Iphicrates replied, 'Very good: if
you, who are Aristophon, would not betray the fleet, would I, who
am Iphicrates?' Only, it must be recognized beforehand that the

other man is more likely than you are to commit the crime in question. Otherwise you will make yourself ridiculous; if it is Aristeides who is prosecuting, you cannot say that sort of thing to him. The purpose is to discredit the prosecutor, who as a rule would have it appear that his character is better than that of the defendant, a pretension which it is desirable to upset. But the use of such an argument is in all cases ridiculous if you are attacking others for what you do or would do yourself, or are urging others to do what you neither do nor would do yourself.

7. Another line of proof is secured by defining your terms. Thus, 'What is the supernatural? Surely it is either a god or the work of a god. Well, any one who believes that the work of a god exists, cannot help also believing that gods exist.' Or take the argument of Iphicrates, 'Goodness is true nobility; neither Harmodius nor Aristogeiton had any nobility before they did a noble deed'. He also argued that he himself was more akin to Harmodius and Aristogeiton than his opponent was. 'At any rate, my deeds are more akin to those of Harmodius and Aristogeiton than yours are'. Another example may be found in the *Alexander*. 'Every one will agree that by incontinent people we mean those who are not satisfied with the enjoyment of one love.' A further example is to be found in the reason given by Socrates for not going to the court of Archelaus. He said that 'one is *insulted* by being unable to requite benefits, as well as by being unable to requite injuries'. All the persons mentioned define their term and get at its essential meaning, and then use the result when reasoning on the point at issue.

8. Another line of argument is founded upon the various senses of a word. Such a word is 'rightly', as has been explained in the *Topics*.

9. Another line is based upon logical division. Thus, 'All men do wrong from one of three motives, A, B, or C: in my case A and B are out of the question, and even the accusers do not allege C'.

10. Another line is based upon induction. Thus from the case of the woman of Peparethus it might be argued that women everywhere can settle correctly the facts about their children. Another example of this occurred at Athens in the case between the orator 1398ᵇ Mantias and his son, when the boy's mother revealed the true facts: and yet another at Thebes, in the case between Ismenias and Stilbon, when Dodonis proved that it was Ismenias who was the father of her son Thettaliscus, and he was in consequence always regarded as being so. A further instance of induction may be taken from the *Law* of Theodectes: 'If we do not hand over our horses to

the care of men who have mishandled other people's horses, nor
ships to those who have wrecked other people's ships, and if this is
true of everything else alike, then men who have failed to secure
other people's safety are not to be employed to secure our own.'
Another instance is the argument of Alcidamas: 'Every one hon-
10   ours the wise'. Thus the Parians have honoured Archilochus, in
spite of his bitter tongue; the Chians Homer, though he was not
their countryman; the Mytilenaeans Sappho, though she was a
woman; the Lacedaemonians actually made Chilon a member of
their senate, though they are the least literary of men; the Italian
Greeks honoured Pythagoras; the inhabitants of Lampsacus gave
15   public burial to Anaxagoras, though he was an alien, and honour
him even to this day. (It may be argued that peoples for whom
philosophers legislate are always prosperous) on the ground that
the Athenians became prosperous under Solon's laws and the
Lacedaemonians under those of Lycurgus, while at Thebes no
sooner did the leading men become philosophers than the country began to prosper.

11. Another line of argument is founded upon some decision already pronounced, whether on the same subject or on one like it
20   or contrary to it. Such a proof is most effective if every one has always decided thus; but if not every one, then at any rate most people; or if all, or most, wise or good men have thus decided, or the
actual judges of the present question, or those whose authority they
accept, or any one whose decision they cannot gainsay because he
has complete control over them, or those whom it is not seemly to
gainsay, as the gods, or one's father, or one's teachers. Thus
Autocles said, when attacking Mixidemides, that it was a strange
25   thing that the Dread Goddesses could without loss of dignity submit to the judgement of the Areopagus, and yet Mixidemides could
not. Or as Sappho said, 'Death is an evil thing; the gods have so
judged it, or they would die'. Or again as Aristippus said in reply to
Plato when he spoke somewhat too dogmatically, as Aristippus
30   thought: 'Well, anyhow, our *friend*,' meaning Socrates, 'never
spoke like that'. And Hegesippus, having previously consulted
Zeus at Olympia, asked Apollo at Delphi 'whether his opinion was
1399ᵃ the same as his father's', implying that it would be shameful for
him to contradict his father. Thus too Isocrates argued that Helen
must have been a good woman, because Theseus decided that she
was; and Paris a good man, because the goddesses chose him before all others; and Evagoras also, says Isocrates, was good, since
5   when Conon met with his misfortune he betook himself to
Evagoras without trying any one else on the way.

12. Another line of argument consists in taking separately the parts of a subject. Such is that given in the *Topics:* 'What *sort* of motion is the soul? for it must be this or that.' The *Socrates* of Theodectes provides an example: 'What temple has he profaned? What gods recognized by the state has he not honoured?'

13. Since it happens that any given thing usually has both good and bad consequences, another line of argument consists in using those consequences as a reason for urging that a thing should or should not be done, for prosecuting or defending any one, for eulogy or censure. E.g. education leads both to unpopularity, which is bad, and to wisdom, which is good. Hence you either argue, 'It is therefore not well to be educated, since it is not well to be unpopular': or you answer, 'No, it is well to be educated, since it is well to be wise'. The *Art of Rhetoric* of Callippus is made up of this line of argument, with the addition of those of Possibility and the others of that kind already described.

14. Another line of argument is used when we have to urge or discourage a course of action that may be done in either of two opposite ways, and have to apply the method just mentioned to both. The difference between this one and the last is that, whereas in the last any two things are contrasted, here the things contrasted are opposites. For instance, the priestess enjoined upon her son not to take to public speaking: 'For', she said, 'if you say what is right, men will hate you; if you say what is wrong, the gods will hate you.' The reply might be, 'On the contrary, you *ought* to take to public speaking: for if you say what is right, the gods will love you; if you say what is wrong, men will love you.' This amounts to the proverbial 'buying the marsh with the salt'. It is just this situation, viz. when each of two opposites has both a good and a bad consequence opposite respectively to each other, that has been termed *divarication*.

15. Another line of argument is this: The things people approve of openly are not those which they approve of secretly: openly, their chief praise is given to justice and nobleness; but in their hearts they prefer their own advantage. Try, in face of this, to establish the point of view which your opponent has not adopted. This is the most effective of the forms of argument that contradict common opinion.

16. Another line is that of rational correspondence. E.g. Iphicrates, when they were trying to compel his son, a youth under the prescribed age, to perform one of the state duties because he was tall, said 'If you count tall boys men, you will next

1399ᵇ be voting short men boys'. And Theodectes in his *Law* said, 'You make citizens of such mercenaries as Strabax and Charidemus, as a reward of their merits; will you not make exiles of such citizens as those who have done irreparable harm among the mercenaries?'

17. Another line is the argument that if two results are the same
5 their antecedents are also the same. For instance, it was a saying of Xenophanes that to assert that the gods had birth is as impious as to say that they die; the consequence of both statements is that there is a time when the gods do not exist. This line of proof assumes generally that the result of any given thing is always the same: e.g. 'you are going to decide not about Isocrates, but about
10 the value of the whole profession of philosophy.' Or, 'to give earth and water' means slavery; or, 'to share in the Common Peace' means obeying orders. We are to make either such assumptions or their opposite, as suits us best.

18. Another line of argument is based on the fact that men do not always make the same choice on a later as on an earlier occasion, but reverse their previous choice. E.g. the following en-
15 thymeme: 'When we were exiles, we fought in order to return; now we have returned, it would be strange to choose exile in order not to have to fight.' On one occasion, that is, they chose to be true to their homes at the cost of fighting, and on the other to avoid fighting at the cost of deserting their homes.

19. Another line of argument is the assertion that some *possible* motive for an event or state of things is the *real* one: e.g. that a gift
20 was given in order to cause pain by its withdrawal. This notion underlies the lines:

> God gives to many great prosperity,
> Not of good will towards them, but to make
> The ruin of them more conspicuous.

25 Or take the passage from the *Meleager* of Antiphon:

> To slay no boar, but to be witnesses
> Of Meleager's prowess unto Greece.

Or the argument in the *Ajax* of Theodectes, that Diomede chose out Odysseus not to do him honour, but in order that his companion might be a lesser man than himself—such a motive for
30 doing so is quite possible.

20. Another line of argument is common to forensic and deliberative oratory, namely, to consider inducements and deterrents, and the motives people have for doing or avoiding the actions in

question. These are the conditions which make us bound to act if they are for us, and to refrain from action if they are against us: that is, we are bound to act if the action is possible, easy, and useful to ourselves or our friends or hurtful to our enemies; this is true even   35
if the action entails loss, provided the loss is outweighed by the solid advantage. A speaker will urge action by pointing to such conditions, and discourage it by pointing to the opposite. These same arguments also form the materials for accusation or defence—the 1400ᵃ
deterrents being pointed out by the defence, and the inducements by the prosecution. As for the defence, . . . This topic forms the whole *Art of Rhetoric* both of Pamphilus and of Callippus.

21. Another line of argument refers to things which are sup-   5
posed to happen and yet seem incredible. We may argue that people could not have believed them, if they had not been true or nearly true: even that they are the more likely to be true because they are incredible. For the things which men believe are either facts or probabilities: if, therefore, a thing that *is* believed is improbable and even incredible, it must be true, since it is certainly not believed because it is at all probable or credible. An example is what Androcles of the deme Pitthus said in his well-known arraignment of the law. The audience tried to shout him down when he observed that the laws required a law to set them right.   10
'Why', he went on, 'fish need salt, improbable and incredible as this might seem for creatures reared in salt water; and olive-cakes need oil, incredible as it is that what produces oil should need it.'

22. Another line of argument is to refute our opponent's case by   15
noting any contrasts or contradictions of dates, acts, or words that it anywhere displays; and this in any of the three following connexions. (1) Referring to our opponent's conduct, e.g. 'He says he is devoted to you, yet he conspired with the Thirty.' (2) Referring to our own conduct, e.g. 'He says I am litigious, and yet he cannot prove that I have been engaged in a single lawsuit.' (3) Referring   20
to both of us together, e.g. '*He* has never even *lent* any one a penny, but I have *ransomed* quite a number of you.'

23. Another line that is useful for men and causes that have been really or seemingly slandered, is to show why the facts are not as supposed; pointing out that there is a reason for the false impression given. Thus a woman, who had palmed off her son on   25
another woman, was thought to be the lad's mistress because she embraced him; but when her action was explained the charge was shown to be groundless. Another example is from the *Ajax* of Theodectes, where Odysseus tells Ajax the reason why, though he is really braver than Ajax, he is not thought so.

24. Another line of argument is to show that if the *cause* is present, the *effect* is present, and if absent, absent. For by proving the
30   cause you at once prove the effect, and conversely nothing can
exist without its cause. Thus Thrasybulus accused Leodamas of
having had his name recorded as a criminal on the slab in the
Acropolis, and of erasing the record in the time of the Thirty
Tyrants: to which Leodamas replied, 'Impossible: for the Thirty
would have trusted me all the more if my quarrel with the com-
35   mons had been inscribed on the slab.'

25. Another line is to consider whether the accused person can
take or could have taken a better course than that which he is rec-
1400ᵇ ommending or taking, or has taken. If he has *not* taken this better
course, it is clear that he is not guilty, since no one deliberately
and consciously chooses what is bad. This argument is, however,
fallacious, for it often becomes clear after the event how the action
could have been done better, though before the event this was far
from clear.

26. Another line is, when a contemplated action is inconsistent
5   with any past action, to examine them both together. Thus, when
the people of Elea asked Xenophanes if they should or should not
sacrifice to Leucothea and mourn for her, he advised them not to
mourn for her if they thought her a goddess, and not to sacrifice
to her if they thought her a mortal woman.

27. Another line is to make previous mistakes the grounds of accusation or defence. Thus, in the *Medea* of Carcinus the accusers
10   allege that Medea has slain her children; 'at all events', they say,
'they are not to be seen'—Medea having made the mistake of
sending her children away. In defence she argues that it is not her
children, but Jason, whom she would have slain; for it would have
been a mistake on her part not to do this if she *had* done the other.
15   This special line of argument for enthymeme forms the whole of
the *Art of Rhetoric* in use before Theodorus.

28. Another line is to draw meanings from names. Sophocles,
for instance, says,

O steel in heart as thou art steel in name.

This line of argument is common in praises of the gods. Thus, too,
Conon called Thrasybulus *rash in counsel*. And Herodicus said of
20   Thrasymachus, 'You are always *bold in battle*'; of Polus, 'you are
always *a colt*'; and of the legislator Draco that his laws were those
not of a human being but of a *dragon*, so savage were they. And,
in Euripides, Hecuba says of Aphrodite,

Her name and Folly's (ἀφροσύνης) rightly begin alike,

and Chaeremon writes

Pentheus—a name foreshadowing grief (πένθος) to come.

The Refutative Enthymeme has a greater reputation than the   25
Demonstrative, because within a small space it works out two opposing arguments, and arguments put side by side are clearer to
the audience. But of all syllogisms, whether refutative or demonstrative, those are most applauded of which we foresee the con-   30
clusions from the beginning, so long as they are not obvious at first
sight—for part of the pleasure we feel is at our own intelligent an-
ticipation; or those which we follow well enough to see the point
of them as soon as the last word has been uttered.

Chapter 24

Besides genuine syllogisms, there may be syllogisms that look genuine but are not; and since an enthymeme is merely a syllogism   35
of a particular kind, it follows that, besides genuine enthymemes,
there may be those that look genuine but are not.

1. Among the lines of argument that form the Spurious
Enthymeme the first is that which arises from the particular words   1401ᵃ
employed.

(a) One variety of this is when—as in dialectic, without having
gone through any reasoning process, we make a final statement as
if it were the conclusion of such a process, 'Therefore so-and-so is
not true', 'Therefore also so-and-so must be true'—so too in rhetoric
a compact and antithetical utterance passes for an enthymeme,   5
such language being the proper province of enthymeme, so that it
is seemingly the form of wording here that causes the illusion mentioned. In order to produce the effect of genuine reasoning by our
form of wording it is useful to summarize the results of a number of
previous reasonings: as 'some he saved—others he avenged—the
Greeks he freed'. Each of these statements has been previously
proved from other facts; but the mere collocation of them gives the   10
impression of establishing some fresh conclusion.

(b) Another variety is based on the use of similar words for different things; e.g. the argument that the mouse must be a noble
creature, since it gives its name to the most august of all religious
rites—for such the Mysteries are. Or one may introduce, into a   15
eulogy of the dog, the dog-star; or Pan, because Pindar said:

> O thou blessed one!
> Thou whom they of Olympus call
> The hound of manifold shape
> That follows the Mother of Heaven:

or we may argue that, because there is much disgrace in there *not*
being a dog about, there is honour in *being* a dog. Or that Hermes
is readier than any other god to go shares, since we never say
'shares all round' except of him. Or that speech is a very excellent
thing, since good men are not said to be worth money but to be
worthy of esteem—the phrase 'worthy of esteem' also having the
meaning of 'worth speech'.

2. Another line is to assert of the whole what is true of the
parts, or of the parts what is true of the whole. A whole and its
parts are supposed to be identical, though often they are not. You
have therefore to adopt whichever of these two lines better suits
your purpose. That is how Euthydemus argues: e.g. that any one
knows that there is a trireme in the Peiraeus, since he knows the
separate details that make up this statement. There is also the argument that one who knows the letters knows the whole word,
since the word is the same thing as the letters which compose it;
or that, if a double portion of a certain thing is harmful to health,
then a single portion must not be called wholesome, since it is
absurd that two good things should make one bad thing. Put
thus, the enthymeme is refutative; put as follows, demonstrative:
'For one good thing cannot be made up of two bad things.' The
whole line of argument is fallacious. Again, there is Polycrates'
saying that Thrasybulus put down thirty tyrants, where the
speaker adds them up one by one. Or the argument in the
Orestes of Theodectes, where the argument is from part to
whole:

> 'Tis right that she who slays her lord should die.

'It is right, too, that the son should avenge his father. Very good:
these two things are what Orestes has done.' Still, perhaps the two
things, once they are put together, do not form a right act. The fallacy might also be said to be due to omission, since the speaker
fails to say by whose hand a husband-slayer should die.

3. Another line is the use of indignant language, whether to support your own case or to overthrow your opponent's. We do this
when we paint a highly-coloured picture of the situation without
having proved the facts of it: if the defendant does so, he produces
an impression of his innocence; and if the prosecutor goes into a

passion, he produces an impression of the defendant's guilt. Here there is no genuine enthymeme: the hearer infers guilt or innocence, but no proof is given, and the inference is fallacious accordingly.

4. Another line is to use a 'Sign', or single instance, as certain evidence; which, again, yields no valid proof. Thus, it might be said that lovers are useful to their countries, since the love of Harmodius and Aristogeiton caused the downfall of the tyrant Hipparchus. Or, again, that Dionysius is a thief, since he is a vicious man — there is, of course, no valid proof here; not every vicious man is a thief, though every thief is a vicious man.

5. Another line represents the accidental as essential. An instance is what Polycrates says of the mice, that they 'came to the rescue' because they gnawed through the bowstrings. Or it might be maintained that an invitation to dinner is a great honour, for it was because he was *not* invited that Achilles was 'angered' with the Greeks at Tenedos. As a fact, what angered him was the *insult* involved; it was a mere accident that this was the particular form that the insult took.

6. Another is the argument from consequence. In the *Alexander,* for instance, it is argued that Paris must have had a lofty disposition, since he despised society and lived by himself on Mount Ida: because lofty people do this kind of thing, therefore Paris too, we are to suppose, had a lofty soul. Or, if a man dresses fashionably and roams around at night, he is a rake, since that is the way rakes behave. Another similar argument points out that beggars sing and dance in temples, and that exiles can live wherever they please, and that such privileges are at the disposal of those we account happy; and therefore every one might be regarded as happy if only he has those privileges. What matters, however, is the *circumstances* under which the privileges are enjoyed. Hence this line too falls under the head of fallacies by omission.

7. Another line consists in representing as causes things which are not causes, on the ground that they happened along with or before the event in question. They assume that, because B happens *after* A, it happens *because* of A. Politicians are especially fond of taking this line. Thus Demades said that the policy of Demosthenes was the cause of all the mischief, 'for after it the war occurred'.

8. Another line consists in leaving out any mention of time and circumstances. E.g. the argument that Paris was justified in taking Helen, since her father left her free to choose: here the freedom

was presumably not perpetual; it could only refer to her first
1402ª choice, beyond which her father's authority could not go. Or
again, one might say that to strike a free man is an act of wanton
outrage; but it is not so in every case—only when it is unprovoked.

9. Again, a spurious syllogism may, as in 'eristical' discussions,
be based on the confusion of the absolute with that which is not
absolute but particular. As, in dialectic, for instance, it may be ar-
5 gued that what-is-not *is*, on the ground that what-is-not *is* what-is-
not; or that the unknown can be known, on the ground that it can
be known to *be* unknown: so also in rhetoric a spurious enthymeme may be based on the confusion of some particular probability with absolute probability. Now no particular probability is
universally probable: as Agathon says,

10   One might perchance say that was probable—
        That things improbable oft will hap to men.

For what is improbable does happen, and therefore it is probable
that improbable things *will* happen. Granted this, one might argue
that 'what is improbable is probable'. But this is not true absolutely.
15 As, in eristic, the imposture comes from not adding any clause
specifying relationship or reference or manner; so here it arises because the probability in question is not general but specific. It is of
this line of argument that Corax's *Art of Rhetoric* is composed. If
the accused is not open to the charge—for instance if a weakling
20 be tried for violent assault—the defence is that he was not likely to
do such a thing. But if he *is* open to the charge—i.e. if he is a *strong*
man—the defence is still that he was not likely to do such a thing,
since he could be sure that people would think he *was* likely to do
it. And so with any other charge: the accused must be either open
or not open to it: there is in either case an appearance of probable
innocence, but whereas in the latter case the probability is genuine, in the former it can only be asserted in the special sense mentioned. This sort of argument illustrates what is meant by making
the worse argument seem the better. Hence people were right in
25 objecting to the training Protagoras undertook to give them. It was
a fraud; the probability it handled was not genuine but spurious,
and has a place in no art except Rhetoric and Eristic.

Chapter 25

Enthymemes, genuine and apparent, have now been described;
30 the next subject is their Refutation.

An argument may be refuted either by a counter-syllogism or by bringing an objection. It is clear that counter-syllogisms can be built up from the same lines of arguments as the original syllogisms: for the materials of syllogisms are the ordinary opinions of men, and such opinions often contradict each other. Objections, as appears in the *Topics*, may be raised in four ways—either by directly attacking your opponent's own statement, or by putting forward another statement like it, or by putting forward a statement contrary to it, or by quoting previous decisions.

1. By 'attacking your opponent's own statement' I mean, for instance, this: if his enthymeme should assert that love is always good, the objection can be brought in two ways, either by making the general statement that 'all want is an evil', or by making the particular one that there would be no talk of 'Caunian love' if there were not evil loves as well as good ones.

2. An objection 'from a contrary statement' is raised when, for instance, the opponent's enthymeme having concluded that a good man does good to all his friends, you object, 'That proves nothing, for a bad man does not do evil to all his friends'.

3. An example of an objection 'from a like statement' is, the enthymeme having shown that ill-used men always hate their ill-users, to reply, 'That proves nothing, for well-used men do not always love those who used them well'.

4. The 'decisions' mentioned are those proceeding from well-known men; for instance, if the enthymeme employed has concluded that 'Some allowance ought to be made for drunken offenders, since they did not know what they were doing', the objection will be, 'Pittacus, then, deserves no approval, or he would not have prescribed specially severe penalties for offences due to drunkenness'.

Enthymemes are based upon one or other of four kinds of alleged fact: (1) Probabilities, (2) Examples, (3) Infallible Signs, (4) Ordinary Signs. (1) Enthymemes based upon Probabilities are those which argue from what is, or is supposed to be, usually true. (2) Enthymemes based upon Example are those which proceed by induction from one or more similar cases, arrive at a general proposition, and then argue deductively to a particular inference. (3) Enthymemes based upon Infallible Signs are those which argue from the inevitable and invariable. (4) Enthymemes based upon ordinary Signs are those which argue from some universal or particular proposition, true or false.

Now (1) as a Probability is that which happens usually but not

always. Enthymemes founded upon Probabilities can, it is clear,
always be refuted by raising some objection. The refutation is not
always genuine: it may be spurious: for it consists in showing not
25   that your opponent's premiss is not probable, but only in showing
that it is not inevitably true. Hence it is always in defence rather
than in accusation that it is possible to gain an advantage by using
this fallacy. For the accuser uses probabilities to prove his case:
and to refute a conclusion as improbable is not the same thing as
to refute it as not inevitable. Any argument based upon what usually happens is always open to objection: otherwise it would not be
30   a probability but an invariable and necessary truth. But the judges
think, if the refutation takes this form, either that the accuser's
case is not probable or that they must not decide it; which, as we
said, is a false piece of reasoning. For they ought to decide by considering not merely what *must* be true but also what is *likely* to be
true: this is, indeed, the meaning of 'giving a verdict in accordance
with one's honest opinion'. Therefore it is not enough for the defendant to refute the accusation by proving that the charge is not
bound to be true: he must do so by showing that it is not *likely* to
35   be true. For this purpose his objection must state what is more
usually true than the statement attacked. It may do so in either of
two ways: either in respect of frequency or in respect of exactness.
It will be most convincing if it does so in both respects; for if the
1403ᵃ thing in question *both* happens *oftener* as we represent it *and* happens more *as* we represent it, the probability is particularly great.

(2) Fallible Signs, and Enthymemes based upon them, can be
refuted even if the facts are correct, as was said at the outset. For
we have shown in the *Analytics* that no Fallible Sign can form part
of a valid logical proof.

5   (3) Enthymemes depending on examples may be refuted in the
same way as probabilities. If we have a negative instance, the argument is refuted, in so far as it is proved not inevitable, even
though the positive examples are more similar and more frequent.
And if the positive examples *are* more numerous and more frequent, we must contend that the present case is dissimilar, or that
its conditions are dissimilar, or that it is different in some way or
other.

10   (4) It will be impossible to refute Infallible Signs, and Enthymemes resting on them, by showing in any way that they do not
form a valid logical proof: this, too, we see from the *Analytics*. All
we can do is to show that the fact alleged does not exist. If there is
15   no doubt that it does, and that it is an Infallible Sign, refutation

now becomes impossible: for this is equivalent to a demonstration which is clear in every respect.

Chapter 26

Amplification and Depreciation are not an element of enthymeme. By 'an element of enthymeme' I mean the same thing
as 'a line of enthymematic argument'—a general class embracing
a large number of particular kinds of enthymeme. Amplification
and Depreciation are one kind of enthymeme, viz. the kind used   20
to show that a thing is great or small; just as there are other kinds
used to show that a thing is good or bad, just or unjust, and anything else of the sort. All these things are the *subject-matter* of syllogisms and enthymemes; none of these is the line of argument of
an enthymeme; no more, therefore, are Amplification and
Depreciation.

Nor are Refutative Enthymemes a different species from   25
Constructive. For it is clear that refutation consists either in offering positive proof or in raising an objection. In the first case we
prove the opposite of our adversary's statements. Thus, if he shows
that a thing has happened, we show that it has not; if he shows that
it has not happened, we show that it has. This, then, could not be
the distinction if there were one, since the same means are em-   30
ployed by both parties, enthymemes being adduced to show that
the fact is or is not so-and-so. An objection, on the other hand, is
not an enthymeme at all, as was said in the *Topics*, it consists
in stating some accepted opinion from which it will be clear that
our opponent has not reasoned correctly or has made a false
assumption.

Three points must be studied in making a speech; and we have
now completed the account of (1) Examples, Maxims,   35
Enthymemes, and in general the *thought*-element—the way to
invent and refute arguments. We have next to discuss (2) Style,   1403ᵇ
and (3) Arrangement.

BOOK III

Chapter 1

IN making a speech one must study three points: first, the means of producing persuasion; second, the style, or language, to be used; third, the proper arrangement of the various parts of the speech. We have already specified the sources of persuasion. We have shown that these are three in number; what they are; and why there are only these three: for we have shown that persuasion must in every case be effected either (1) by working on the emotions of the judges themselves, (2) by giving them the right impression of the speakers' character, or (3) by proving the truth of the statements made.

Enthymemes also have been described, and the sources from which they should be derived; there being both special and general lines of argument for enthymemes.

Our next subject will be the style of expression. For it is not enough to know *what* we ought to say; we must also say it *as* we ought; much help is thus afforded towards producing the right impression of a speech. The first question to receive attention was naturally the one that comes first naturally—how persuasion can be produced from the facts themselves. The second is how to set these facts out in language. A third would be the proper method of delivery; this is a thing that affects the success of a speech greatly; but hitherto the subject has been neglected. Indeed, it was long before it found a way into the arts of tragic drama and epic recitation: at first poets acted their tragedies themselves. It is plain that delivery has just as much to do with oratory as with poetry. (In connexion with poetry, it has been studied by Glaucon of Teos among others.) It is, essentially, a matter of the right management of the voice to express the various emotions—of speaking loudly, softly, or between the two; of high, low, or intermediate pitch; of the various rhythms that suit various subjects. These are the three things—volume of sound, modulation of pitch, and rhythm—that a speaker bears in mind. It is those who *do* bear them in mind who

119

usually win prizes in the dramatic contests; and just as in drama
the actors now count for more than the poets, so it is in the con-
35 tests of public life, owing to the defects of our political institutions.
No systematic treatise upon the rules of delivery has yet been composed; indeed, even the study of language made no progress till
late in the day. Besides, delivery is—very properly—not regarded
1404ᵃ as an elevated subject of inquiry. Still, the whole business of
rhetoric being concerned with appearances, we must pay attention to the subject of delivery, unworthy though it is, because we
cannot do without it. The right thing in speaking really is that we
should be satisfied not to annoy our hearers, without trying to de-
5   light them: we ought in fairness to fight our case with no help beyond the bare facts: nothing, therefore, should matter except the
proof of those facts. Still, as has been already said, other things affect the result considerably, owing to the defects of our hearers.
The arts of language cannot help having a small but real importance, whatever it is we have to expound to others: the way in
10 which a thing is said does affect its intelligibility. Not, however, so
much importance as people think. All such arts are fanciful and
meant to charm the hearer. Nobody uses fine language when
teaching geometry.

When the principles of delivery have been worked out, they will
produce the same effect as on the stage. But only very slight at-
tempts to deal with them have been made and by a few people, as
15 by Thrasymachus in his 'Appeals to Pity'. Dramatic ability is a natural gift, and can hardly be systematically taught. The principles
of good diction can be so taught, and therefore we have men of
ability in this direction too, who win prizes in their turn, as well as
those speakers who excel in delivery—speeches of the written or
literary kind owe more of their effect to their direction than to
their thought.

20   It was naturally the poets who first set the movement going; for
words represent things, and they had also the human voice at their
disposal, which of all our organs can best represent other things.
Thus the arts of recitation and acting were formed, and others as
well. Now it was because poets seemed to win fame through their
fine language when their thoughts were simple enough, that the
25 language of oratorical prose at first took a poetical colour, e.g. that
of Gorgias. Even now most uneducated people think that poetical
language makes the finest discourses. That is not true: the language of prose is distinct from that of poetry. This is shown by the
state of things to-day, when even the language of tragedy has al-
30 tered its character. Just as iambics were adopted, instead of tetram-

eters, because they are the most prose-like of all metres, so tragedy
has given up all those words, not used in ordinary talk, which dec-
orated the early drama and are still used by the writers of hexam-
eter poems. It is therefore ridiculous to imitate a poetical manner   35
which the poets themselves have dropped; and it is now plain that
we have not to treat in detail the whole question of style, but may
confine ourselves to that part of it which concerns our present subject, rhetoric. The other—the poetical—part of it has been discussed in the treatise on the *Art of Poetry*.

Chapter 2

We may, then, start from the observations there made, including   1404ᵇ
the definition of style. Style to be good must be clear, as is proved
by the fact that speech which fails to convey a plain meaning will
fail to do just what speech has to do. It must also be appropriate,
avoiding both meanness and undue elevation; poetical language is
certainly free from meanness, but it is not appropriate to prose.   5
Clearness is secured by using the words (nouns and verbs alike)
that are current and ordinary. Freedom from meanness, and positive adornment too, are secured by using the other words mentioned in the *Art of Poetry*. Such variation from what is usual
makes the language appear more stately. People do not feel towards strangers as they do towards their own countrymen, and the   10
same thing is true of their feeling for language. It is therefore well
to give to everyday speech an unfamiliar air: people like what
strikes them, and are struck by what is out of the way. In verse such
effects are common, and there they are fitting: the persons and
things there spoken of are comparatively remote from ordinary
life. In prose passages they are far less often fitting because the   15
subject-matter is less exalted. Even in poetry, it is not quite appropriate that fine language should be used by a slave or a very young
man, or about very trivial subjects: even in poetry the style, to be
appropriate, must sometimes be toned down, though at other
times heightened. We can now see that a writer must disguise his
art and give the impression of speaking naturally and not artifi-
cially. Naturalness is persuasive, artificiality is the contrary; for our   20
hearers are prejudiced and think we have some design against
them, as if we were mixing their wines for them. It is like the difference between the quality of Theodorus' voice and the voices of
all other actors: his really seems to be that of the character who is
speaking, theirs do not. We can hide our purpose successfully by

taking the single words of our composition from the speech of or-
25   dinary life. This is done in poetry by Euripides, who was the first
to show the way to his successors.

Language is composed of nouns and verbs. Nouns are of the
various kinds considered in the treatise on Poetry. Strange words,
compound words, and invented words must be used sparingly and
30   on few occasions: on *what* occasions we shall state later. The reason for this restriction has been already indicated: they depart
from what is suitable, in the direction of excess. In the language
of prose, besides the regular and proper terms for things,
metaphorical terms only can be used with advantage. This we
gather from the fact that these two classes of terms, the proper or
regular and the metaphorical—these and no others—are used by
35   everybody in conversation. We can now see that a good writer can
produce a style that is distinguished without being obtrusive, and
is at the same time clear, thus satisfying our definition of good oratorical prose. Words of ambiguous meaning are chiefly useful to
enable the sophist to mislead his hearers. Synonyms are useful to
the poet, by which I mean words whose ordinary meaning is the
1405ª same, e.g. πορεύεσθαι (*advancing*) and βαδίξειν (*proceeding*);
these two are ordinary words and have the same meaning.

In the *Art of Poetry*, as we have already said, will be found definitions of these kinds of words; a classification of Metaphors; and
mention of the fact that metaphor is of great value both in poetry
5   and in prose. Prose-writers must, however, pay specially careful attention to metaphor, because their other resources are scantier
than those of poets. Metaphor, moreover, gives style clearness,
charm, and distinction as nothing else can: and it is not a thing
whose use can be taught by one man to another. Metaphors, like
10   epithets, must be fitting, which means that they must fairly correspond to the thing signified: failing this, their inappropriateness
will be conspicuous: the want of harmony between two things is
emphasized by their being placed side by side. It is like having to
ask ourselves what dress will suit an old man; certainly not the
crimson cloak that suits a young man. And if you wish to pay a
15   compliment, you must take your metaphor from something better
in the same line; if to disparage, from something worse. To illus-
trate my meaning: since opposites are in the same class, you do
what I have suggested if you say that a man who begs 'prays', and
a man who prays 'begs'; for praying and begging are both varieties
20   of asking. So Iphicrates called Callias a 'mendicant priest' instead
of a 'torch-bearer', and Callias replied that Iphicrates must be
uninitiated or he would have called him not a 'mendicant priest'

but a 'torch-bearer'. Both are religious titles, but one is honourable and the other is not. Again, somebody calls actors
'hangers-on of Dionysus', but they call themselves 'artists': each of
these terms is a metaphor, the one intended to throw dirt at the   25
actor, the other to dignify him. And pirates now call themselves
'purveyors'. We can thus call a crime a mistake, or a mistake a
crime. We can say that a thief 'took' a thing, or that he 'plundered'
his victim. An expression like that of Euripides' Telephus,

> King of the oar, on Mysia's coast he landed,

is inappropriate; the word 'king' goes beyond the dignity of the   30
subject, and so the art is *not* concealed. A metaphor may be amiss
because the very syllables of the words conveying it fail to indicate
sweetness of vocal utterance. Thus Dionysius the Brazen in his
elegies calls poetry 'Calliope's screech'. Poetry and screeching are
both, to be sure, vocal utterances. But the metaphor is bad, because the sounds of 'screeching', unlike those of poetry, are dis-
cordant and unmeaning. Further, in using metaphors to give
names to nameless things, we must draw them not from remote
but from kindred and similar things, so that the kinship is clearly   35
perceived as soon as the words are said. Thus in the celebrated
riddle

> I marked how a man glued bronze with fire to another man's body,   1405ᵇ

the process is nameless; but both it and gluing are a kind of application, and that is why the application of the cupping-glass is here
called a 'gluing'. Good riddles do, in general, provide us with satisfactory metaphors: for metaphors imply riddles, and therefore a   5
good riddle can furnish a good metaphor. Further, the materials
of metaphors must be beautiful; and the beauty, like the ugliness,
of all words may, as Licymnius says, lie in their sound or in their
meaning. Further, there is a third consideration—one that upsets
the fallacious argument of the sophist Bryson, that there is no such
thing as foul language, because in whatever words you put a given   10
thing your meaning is the same. This is untrue. One term may describe a thing more truly than another, may be more like it, and
set it more intimately before our eyes. Besides, two different words
will represent a thing in two different lights; so on this ground also
one term must be held fairer or fouler than another. For both of   15
two terms will indicate what *is* fair, or what *is* foul, but not simply
their fairness or their foulness, or if so, at any rate not in an equal
degree. The materials of metaphor must be beautiful to the ear, to
the understanding, to the eye or some other physical sense. It is

better, for instance, to say 'rosy-fingered morn', than 'crimson-
20 fingered' or, worse still, 'red-fingered morn'. The epithets that we
apply, too, may have a bad and ugly aspect, as when Orestes is
called a 'mother-slayer'; or a better one, as when he is called his
'father's avenger'. Simonides, when the victor in the mule-race of-
fered him a small fee, refused to write him an ode, because, he
25 said, it was so unpleasant to write odes to half-asses: but on receiving an adequate fee, he wrote

Hail to you, daughters of storm-footed steeds,

though of course they were daughters of asses too. The same effect
is attained by the use of diminutives, which make a bad thing less
30 bad and a good thing less good. Take, for instance, the banter of
Aristophanes in the *Babylonians* where he uses 'goldlet' for 'gold',
'cloaklet' for 'cloak', 'scofflet' for 'scoff, and 'plaguelet'. But alike
in using epithets and in using diminutives we must be wary and
must observe the mean.

Chapter 3

Bad taste in language may take any of four forms:—
35   (1) The misuse of compound words. Lycophron, for instance,
talks of the '*many-visaged* heaven' above the '*giant-crested* earth',
1406ª and again the '*strait-pathed* shore'; and Gorgias of the '*pauper-poet*
flatterer' and 'oath-breaking and *over-oath-keeping*'. Alcidamas
uses such expressions as 'the soul filling with rage and face becoming *flame-flushed*', and 'he thought their enthusiasm would be
issue-fraught' and '*issue-fraught* he made the persuasion of his
5 words', and '*sombre-hued* is the floor of the sea'. The way all these
words are compounded makes them, we feel, fit for verse only.
This, then, is one form in which bad taste is shown.
       (2) Another is the employment of strange words. For instance,
Lycophron talks of 'the *prodigious* Xerxes' and '*spoliative* Sciron';
Alcidamas of 'a *toy* for poetry' and 'the *witlessness* of nature', and
10 says '*whetted* with the *unmitigated* temper of his spirit'.
       (3) A third form is the use of long, unseasonable, or frequent ep-
ithets. It is appropriate enough for a poet to talk of 'white milk',
but in prose such epithets are sometimes lacking in appropriateness or, when spread too thickly, plainly reveal the author turning
his prose into poetry. Of course we must use some epithets, since
15 they lift our style above the usual level and give it an air of distinction. But we must aim at the due mean, or the result will be

worse than if we took no trouble at all; we shall get something actually bad instead of something merely not good. That is why the
epithets of Alcidamas seem so tasteless; he does not use them as
the seasoning of the meat, but as the meat itself, so numerous and
swollen and aggressive are they. For instance, he does not say   20
'sweat', but 'the *moist* sweat'; not 'to the Isthmian games', but 'to
the *world-concourse* of the Isthmian games'; not 'laws', but 'the
laws *that are monarchs of states*'; not 'at a run', but '*his heart im-
pelling him to speed of foot*'; not 'a school of the Muses', but
'*Nature's* school of the Muses had he inherited'; and so '*frowning*   25
care of heart', and 'achiever' not of 'popularity' but of '*universal*
popularity', and '*dispenser* of pleasure to his audience', and 'he
concealed it' not 'with boughs' but 'with boughs *of the forest trees*',
and 'he clothed' not 'his body' but '*his body's nakedness*', and 'his   30
soul's desire was *counter-imitative*' (this is at one and the same
time a compound and an epithet, so that it seems a poet's effort),
and 'so *extravagant* the excess of his wickedness'. We thus see how
the inappropriateness of such poetical language imports absurdity
and tastelessness into speeches, as well as the obscurity that comes
from all this verbosity—for when the sense is plain, you only ob-   35
scure and spoil its clearness by piling up words.

The ordinary use of compound words is where there is no term
for a thing and some compound can be easily formed, like 'pas-
time' (χρονοτριβεῖν); but if this is much done, the prose character disappears entirely. We now see why the language of 1406ᵇ
compounds is just the thing for writers of dithyrambs, who love
sonorous noises; strange words for writers of epic poetry, which is
a proud and stately affair; and metaphor for iambic verse, the
metre which (as has been already said) is widely used to-day.

(4) There remains the fourth region in which bad taste may be   5
shown, metaphor. Metaphors like other things may be inappropriate. Some are so because they are ridiculous; they are indeed
used by comic as well as tragic poets. Others are too grand and
theatrical; and these, if they are far-fetched, may also be obscure.
For instance, Gorgias talks of 'events that are green and full of
sap', and says 'foul was the deed you sowed and evil the harvest   10
you reaped'. That is too much like poetry. Alcidamas, again, called
philosophy 'a fortress that threatens the power of law', and the
Odyssey 'a goodly looking-glass of human life', and talked about
'offering no such toy to poetry': all these expressions fail, for the
reasons given, to carry the hearer with them. The address of   15
Gorgias to the swallow, when she had let her droppings fall on
him as she flew overhead, is in the best tragic manner. He said,

'Nay, shame, O Philomela'. Considering her as a bird, you could not call her act shameful; considering her as a girl, you could; and so it was a good gibe to address her as what she was once and not as what she is.

Chapter 4

20   The Simile also is a metaphor; the difference is but slight. When the poet says of Achilles that he

Leapt on the foe as a lion,

this is a simile; when he says of him 'the lion leapt', it is a metaphor—here, since both are courageous, he has transferred to Achilles the name of 'lion'. Similes are useful in prose as well as in verse; but not often, since they are of the nature of poetry. They
25   are to be employed just as metaphors are employed, since they are really the same thing except for the difference mentioned.

The following are examples of similes. Androtion said of Idrieus that he was like a terrier let off the chain, that flies at you and bites
30   you—Idrieus too was savage now that he was let out of *his* chains. Theodamas compared Archidamus to an Euxenus who could not do geometry—a proportional simile, implying that Euxenus is an Archidamus who *can* do geometry. In Plato's *Republic* those who strip the dead are compared to curs which bite the stones thrown at them but do not touch the thrower, and there is the simile
35   about the Athenian people, who are compared to a ship's captain who is strong but a little deaf; and the one about poets' verses, which are likened to persons who lack beauty but possess youthful freshness—when the freshness had faded the charm perishes, and
1407ᵃ so with verses when broken up into prose. Pericles compared the Samians to children who take their pap but go on crying; and the Boeotians to holm-oaks, because they were ruining one another by
5   civil wars just as one oak causes another oak's fall. Demosthenes said that the Athenian people were like sea-sick men on board ship. Again, Democrates compared the political orators to nurses who swallow the bit of food themselves and then smear the children's lips with the spittle. Antisthenes compared the lean
10   Cephisodotus to frankincense, because it was his consumption that gave one pleasure. All these ideas may be expressed either as similes or as metaphors; those which succeed as metaphors will obviously do well also as similes, and similes, with the explanation omitted, will appear as metaphors. But the proportional metaphor

must always apply reciprocally to either of its co-ordinate terms.   15
For instance, if a drinking-bowl is the shield of Dionysus, a shield
may fittingly be called the drinking-bowl of Ares.

Chapter 5

Such, then, are the ingredients of which speech is composed. The
foundation of good style is correctness of language, which falls
under five heads. (1) First, the proper use of connecting words,
and the arrangement of them in the natural sequence which some   20
of them require. For instance, the connective μέν (e.g. ἐγὼ μέν)
requires the correlative δέ (e.g. ὁ δέ). The answering word must
be brought in before the first has been forgotten, and not be
widely separated from it; nor, except in the few cases where this is
appropriate, is another connective to be introduced before the one   25
required. Consider the sentence, 'But I, as soon as he told me (for
Cleon had come begging and praying), took them along and set
out.' In this sentence many connecting words are inserted in front
of the one required to complete the sense; and if there is a long in-
terval before 'set out', the result is obscurity. One merit, then, of
good style lies in the right use of connecting words. (2) The sec-   30
ond lies in calling things by their own special names and not by
vague general ones. (3) The third is to avoid ambiguities; unless,
indeed, you definitely desire to be ambiguous, as those do who
have nothing to say but are pretending to mean something. Such
people are apt to put that sort of thing into verse. Empedocles, for   35
instance, by his long circumlocutions imposes on his hearers;
these are affected in the same way as most people are when they
listen to diviners, whose ambiguous utterances are received with
nods of acquiescence —

> Croesus by crossing the Halys will ruin a mighty realm.

Diviners use these vague generalities about the matter in hand be-   1407ᵇ
cause their predictions are thus, as a rule, less likely to be falsified.
We are more likely to be right, in the game of 'odd and even', if
we simply guess 'even' or 'odd' than if we guess at the actual number; and the oracle-monger is more likely to be right if he simply
says that a thing will happen than if he says *when* it will happen,
and therefore he refuses to add a definite date. All these ambigui-   5
ties have the same sort of effect, and are to be avoided unless we
have some such object as that mentioned. (4) A fourth rule is to
observe Protagoras' classification of nouns into male, female, and

inanimate; for these distinctions also must be correctly given. 'Upon her arrival she said her say and departed (ἡ δ' ἐλθοῦσα καὶ διαλεχθεῖσα ᾤχετο).' (5) A fifth rule is to express plurality, few-10 ness, and unity by the correct wording, e.g. 'Having come, they struck me (οἱ δ' ἐλθόντες ἔτυπτόν με).'

It is a general rule that a written composition should be easy to read and therefore easy to deliver. This cannot be so where there are many connecting words or clauses, or where punctuation is hard, as in the writings of Heracleitus. To punctuate Heracleitus is no easy task, because we often cannot tell whether a particular 15 word belongs to what precedes or what follows it. Thus, at the out-set of his treatise he says, 'Though this truth is always men under-stand it not', where it is not clear with which of the two clauses the word 'always' should be joined by the punctuation. Further, the following fact leads to solecism, viz. that the sentence does not work out properly if you annex to two terms a third which does not 20 suit them both. Thus either 'sound' or 'colour' will fail to work out properly with some verbs: 'perceive' will apply to both, 'see' will not. Obscurity is also caused if, when you intend to insert a num-ber of details, you do not first make your meaning clear; for in-stance, if you say, 'I meant, after telling him this, that, and the other thing, to set out', rather than something of this kind 'I meant 25 to set out after telling him; then this, that, and the other thing occurred.'

Chapter 6

The following suggestions will help to give your language impres-siveness. (1) Describe a thing instead of naming it: do not say 'cir-cle', but 'that surface which extends equally from the middle every way'. To achieve conciseness, do the opposite—put the name instead of the description. When mentioning anything ugly or un-30 seemly, use its name if it is the description that is ugly, and de-scribe it if it is the name that is ugly. (2) Represent things with the help of metaphors and epithets, being careful to avoid poetical ef-fects. (3) Use plural for singular, as in poetry, where one finds

Unto havens Achaean,

though only one haven is meant,
and

Here are my letter's many-leavèd folds.

(4) Do not bracket two words under one article, but put one arti-   35
cle with each; e.g. τῆς γυναικὸς τῆς ἡμετέρας. The reverse to secure conciseness; e.g. τῆς ἡμετέρας γυναικός. (5) Use plenty of
connecting words; conversely, to secure conciseness, dispense
with connectives, while still preserving connexion; e.g. 'having
gone and spoken', and 'having gone, I spoke', respectively. (6) And   1408ᵃ
the practice of Antimachus, too, is useful — to describe a thing by
mentioning attributes it does not possess; as he does in talking of
Teumessus —

> There is a little wind-swept knoll . . .

A subject can be developed indefinitely along these lines. You
may apply this method of treatment by negation either to good or
to bad qualities, according to which your subject requires. It is   5
from this source that the poets draw expressions such as the 'string-
less' or 'lyreless' melody, thus forming epithets out of negations.
This device is popular in proportional metaphors, as when the
trumpet's note is called 'a lyreless melody'.

Chapter 7

Your language will be *appropriate* if it expresses emotion and char-   10
acter, and if it corresponds to its subject. 'Correspondence to subject' means that we must neither speak casually about weighty
matters, nor solemnly about trivial ones; nor must we add orna-
mental epithets to commonplace nouns, or the effect will be
comic, as in the works of Cleophon, who can use phrases as ab-   15
surd as 'O queenly fig-tree'. To express emotion, you will employ
the language of anger in speaking of outrage; the language of dis-
gust and discreet reluctance to utter a word when speaking of
impiety or foulness; the language of exultation for a tale of glory,
and that of humiliation for a tale of pity; and so in all other cases.

   This aptness of language is one thing that makes people believe   20
in the truth of your story: their minds draw the false conclusion
that you are to be trusted from the fact that others behave as you
do when things are as you describe them; and therefore they take
your story to be true, whether it is so or not. Besides, an emotional
speaker always makes his audience feel with him, even when there
is nothing in his arguments; which is why many speakers try to
overwhelm their audience by mere noise.   25
   Furthermore, this way of proving your story by displaying these
signs of its genuineness expresses your personal character. Each

class of men, each type of disposition, will have its own appropriate way of letting the truth appear. Under 'class' I include differences of age, as boy, man, or old man; of sex, as man or woman;
of nationality, as Spartan or Thessalian. By 'dispositions' I here
mean those dispositions only which determine the character of a
30   man's life, for it is not every disposition that does this. If, then, a
speaker uses the very words which are in keeping with a particular
disposition, he will reproduce the corresponding character; for a
rustic and an educated man will not say the same things nor speak
in the same way. Again, some impression is made upon an audience by a device which speech-writers employ to nauseous excess,
when they say 'Who does not know this?' or 'It is known to every
35   body.' The hearer is ashamed of his ignorance, and agrees with the
speaker, so as to have a share of the knowledge that everybody else
possesses.

1408ᵇ   All the variations of oratorical style are capable of being used in
season or out of season. The best way to counteract any exaggeration is the well-worn device by which the speaker puts in some
criticism of himself; for then people feel it must be all right for
him to talk thus, since he certainly knows what he is doing.
Further, it is better not to have everything always just correspond
5   ing to everything else — your hearers will see through you less easily thus. I mean for instance, if your words are harsh, you should
not extend this harshness to your voice and your countenance and
have everything else in keeping. If you do, the artificial character
of each detail becomes apparent; whereas if you adopt one device
and not another, you are using art all the same and yet nobody notices it. (To be sure, if mild sentiments are expressed in harsh tones
and harsh sentiments in mild tones, you become comparatively
10   unconvincing.) Compound words, fairly plentiful epithets, and
strange words best suit an emotional speech. We forgive an angry
man for talking about a wrong as 'heaven-high' or 'colossal'; and
we excuse such language when the speaker has his hearers already
in his hands and has stirred them deeply either by praise or blame
15   or anger or affection, as Isocrates, for instance, does at the end of
his *Panegyric*, with his 'name and fame' and 'in that they brooked'.
Men do speak in this strain when they are deeply stirred, and so,
once the audience is in a like state of feeling, approval of course
follows. This is why such language is fitting in poetry, which is an
inspired thing. This language, then, should be used either under
20   stress of emotion, or ironically, after the manner of Gorgias and of
the passages in the *Phaedrus*.

Chapter 8

The form of a prose composition should be neither metrical nor destitute of rhythm. The metrical form destroys the hearer's trust by its artificial appearance, and at the same time it diverts his attention, making him watch for metrical recurrences, just as children catch up the herald's question, 'Whom does the freedman choose as his advocate?', with the answer 'Cleon!' On the other hand, unrhythmical language is too unlimited; we do not want the limitations of metre, but some limitation we must have, or the effect will be vague and unsatisfactory. Now it is number that limits all things; and it is the numerical limitation of the form of a composition that constitutes rhythm, of which metres are definite sections.

Prose, then, is to be rhythmical, but not metrical, or it will become not prose but verse. It should not even have too precise a prose rhythm, and therefore should only be rhythmical to a certain extent.

Of the various rhythms, the heroic has dignity, but lacks the tones of the spoken language. The iambic is the very language of ordinary people, so that in common talk iambic lines occur oftener than any others: but in a speech we need dignity and the power of taking the hearer out of his ordinary self. The trochee is too much akin to wild dancing: we can see this in tetrameter verse, which is one of the trochaic rhythms.

There remains the paean, which speakers began to use in the time of Thrasymachus, though they had then no name to give it. The paean is a third class of rhythm, closely akin to both the two already mentioned; it has in it the ratio of three to two, whereas the other two kinds have the ratio of one to one, and two to one respectively. Between the two last ratios comes the ratio of one-and-a-half to one, which is that of the paean.

Now the other two kinds of rhythm must be rejected in writing prose, partly for the reasons given, and partly because they are too metrical; and the paean must be adopted, since from this alone of the rhythms mentioned no definite metre arises, and therefore it is the least obtrusive of them. At present the same form of paean is employed at the beginning as at the end of sentences, whereas the end should differ from the beginning. There are two opposite kinds of paean, one of which is suitable to the beginning of a sentence, where it is indeed actually used; this is the kind that begins with a long syllable and ends with three short ones, as

15   Δαλογενὲς | εἴτε Λυκί | αν,

  and

                Χρυσεοκόμ | α Ἑκατε | παῖ Διός.

The other paean begins, conversely, with three short syllables and
ends with a long one, as

          μετὰ δὲ γᾶν | ὕδατά τ᾽ ὠκ | εανὸν ἡ | φάνισε νύξ.

This kind of paean makes a real close: a short syllable can give no
effect of finality, and therefore makes the rhythm appear trun-
cated. A sentence should break off with the long syllable: the fact
20 that it is over should be indicated not by the scribe, or by his
period-mark in the margin, but by the rhythm itself.

We have now seen that our language must be rhythmical and
not destitute of rhythm, and what rhythms, in what particular
shape, make it so.

                          Chapter 9

The language of prose must be either free-running, with its parts
united by nothing except the connecting words, like the preludes
25 in dithyrambs; or compact and antithetical, like the strophes of the
old poets. The free-running style is the ancient one, e.g. 'Herein is
set forth the inquiry of Herodotus the Thurian.' Every one used
this method formerly; not many do so now. By 'free-running' style
I mean the kind that has no natural stopping-places, and comes to
30 a stop only because there is no more to say of that subject. This
style is unsatisfying just because it goes on indefinitely—one always likes to sight a stopping-place in front of one: it is only at the
goal that men in a race faint and collapse; while they see the end
of the course before them, they can keep going. Such, then, is the
free-running kind of style; the compact is that which is in periods.
35 By a period I mean a portion of speech that has in itself a beginning and an end, being at the same time not too big to be taken
1409ᵇ in at a glance. Language of this kind is satisfying and easy to follow. It is satisfying, because it is just the reverse of indefinite; and
moreover, the hearer always feels that he is grasping something
and has reached some definite conclusion; whereas it is unsatisfactory to see nothing in front of you and get nowhere. It is easy to
follow, because it can easily be remembered; and this because lan-
5 guage when in periodic form can be numbered, and number is

the easiest of all things to remember. That is why verse, which is measured, is always more easily remembered than prose, which is not: the measures of verse can be numbered. The period must, further, not be completed until the sense is complete: it must not be capable of breaking off abruptly, as may happen with the following iambic lines of Sophocles —

> Calydon's soil is this; of Pelops' land   10
> (The smiling plains face us across the strait.)

By a wrong division of the words the hearer may take the meaning to be the reverse of what it is: for instance, in the passage quoted, one might imagine that Calydon is in the Peloponnesus.

A Period may be either divided into several members or simple. The period of several members is a portion of speech (1) complete in itself, (2) divided into parts, and (3) easily delivered at a single breath—as a whole, that is; not by fresh breath being taken at the   15 division. A member is one of the two parts of such a period. By a 'simple' period, I mean that which has only one member. The members, and the whole periods, should be neither curt nor long. A member which is too short often makes the listener stumble; he is still expecting the rhythm to go on to the limit his mind has   20 fixed for it; and if meanwhile he is pulled back by the speaker's stopping, the shock is bound to make him, so to speak, stumble. If, on the other hand, you go on too long, you make him feel left behind, just as people who when walking pass beyond the boundary before turning back leave their companions behind. So too if a period is too long you turn it into a speech, or something like a   25 dithyrambic prelude. The result is much like the preludes that Democritus of Chios jeered at Melanippides for writing instead of antistrophic stanzas —

> He that sets traps for another man's feet
>   Is like to fall into them first;
> And long-winded preludes do harm to us all,
>   But the preluder catches it worst.

Which applies likewise to long-membered orators. Periods whose   30 members are altogether too short are not periods at all; and the result is to bring the hearer down with a crash.

The periodic style which is divided into members is of two kinds. It is either simply divided, as in 'I have often wondered at the conveners of national gatherings and the founders of athletic contests'; or it is antithetical, where, in each of the two members,   35 one of one pair of opposites is put along with one of another pair,

1410ᵃ or the same word is used to bracket two opposites, as 'They aided
both parties—not only those who stayed behind but those who accompanied them: for the latter they acquired new territory larger
than that at home, and to the former they left territory at home
that was large enough'. Here the contrasted words are 'staying behind' and 'accompanying', 'enough' and 'larger'. So in the exam-
5   ple, 'Both to those who want to get property and to those who
desire to enjoy it' where 'enjoyment' is contrasted with 'getting'.
Again, 'it often happens in such enterprises that the wise men fail
and the fools succeed'; 'they were awarded the prize of valour im-
mediately, and won the command of the sea not long afterwards';
10   'to sail through the mainland and march through the sea, by
bridging the Hellespont and cutting through Athos'; 'nature gave
them their country and law took it away again'; 'some of them perished in misery, others were saved in disgrace'; 'Athenian citizens
keep foreigners in their houses as servants, while the city of Athens
15   allows her allies by thousands to live as the foreigner's slaves'; and
'to possess in life or to bequeath at death'. There is also what some
one said about Peitholaus and Lycophron in a law-court, 'These
men used to sell you when they were at home, and now they have
come to you here and bought you'. All these passages have the
20   structure described above. Such a form of speech is satisfying, because the significance of contrasted ideas is easily felt, especially
when they are thus put side by side, and also because it has the effect of a logical argument; it is by putting two opposing conclusions side by side that you prove one of them false.

Such, then, is the nature of *antithesis*. *Parisosis* is making the
two members of a period equal in length. *Paromoeosis* is making
the extreme words of both members like each other. This must
25   happen either at the beginning or at the end of each member. If
at the beginning, the resemblance must always be between whole
words; at the end, between final syllables or inflexions of the same
word or the same word repeated. Thus, at the beginning

ἀγρὸν γὰρ ἔλαβεν ἀργὸν παρ' αὐτοῦ

and

δωρητοί τ' ἐπέλοντο παράρρητοί τ' ἐπέεσσιν.

At the end

30   οὐκ ᾠήθησαν αὐτὸν παιδίον τετοκέναι, ἀλλ' αὐτοῦ
αἴτιον γεγονέναι,

and

ἐν πλείσταις δὲ φροντίσι καὶ ἐν ἐλαχίσταις ἐλπίσιν.

An example of inflexions of the same word is

ἄξιος δὲ σταθῆναι χαλκοῦς, οὐκ ἄξιος ὢν χαλκοῦ;

Of the same word repeated,

σὺ δ' αὐτὸν καὶ ζῶνατ ἔλεγες κακῶς καὶ νῦν γράφεις κακῶς.

Of one syllable,

τί δ' ἂν ἔπαθες δεινόν, εἰ ἄνδρ' εἶδες ἀργόν;   35

It is possible for the same sentence to have all these features to-gether—*antithesis, parison,* and *homoeoteleuton.* (The possible 1410ᵇ beginnings of periods have been pretty fully enumerated in the *Theodectea.*) There are also spurious antitheses, like that of Epicharmus—

> There one time I as their guest did stay,
> And they were my hosts on another day.   5

Chapter 10

We may now consider the above points settled, and pass on to say something about the way to devise lively and taking sayings. Their actual invention can only come through natural talent or long practice; but this treatise may indicate the way it is done. We may deal with them by enumerating the different kinds of them. We will begin by remarking that we all naturally find it agreeable to get   10 hold of new ideas easily: words express ideas, and therefore those words are the most agreeable that enable us to get hold of new ideas. Now strange words simply puzzle us; ordinary words convey only what we know already; it is from metaphor that we can best get hold of something fresh. When the poet calls old age 'a with-ered stalk', he conveys a new idea, a new fact, to us by means of the general notion of 'lost bloom', which is common to both things. The similes of the poets do the same, and therefore, if they are   15 good similes, give an effect of brilliance. The simile, as has been said before, is a metaphor, differing from it only in the way it is put; and just because it is longer it is less attractive. Besides, it does not say outright that 'this' *is* 'that', and therefore the hearer is less in-terested in the idea. We see, then, that both speech and reasoning   20 are lively in proportion as they make us seize a new idea promptly. For this reason people are not much taken either by obvious

arguments (using the word 'obvious' to mean what is plain to everybody and needs no investigation), nor by those which puzzle us
when we hear them stated, but only by those which convey their
25　information to us as soon as we hear them, provided we had not the
information already; or which the mind only just fails to keep up
with. These two kinds do convey to us a sort of information: but the
obvious and the obscure kinds convey nothing, either at once or
later on. It is these qualities, then, that, so far as the meaning of
what is said is concerned, make an argument acceptable. So far as
the style is concerned, it is the antithetical form that appeals to us,
30　e.g. 'judging that the peace common to all the rest was a war upon
their own private interests,' where there is an antithesis between
war and peace. It is also good to use metaphorical words; but the
metaphors must not be far-fetched, or they will be difficult to grasp,
nor obvious, or they will have no effect. The words, too, ought to
set the scene before our eyes; for events ought to be seen in
progress rather than in prospect. So we must aim at these three
35　points: Antithesis, Metaphor, and Actuality.
1411ᵃ　　Of the four kinds of Metaphor the most taking is the proportional kind. Thus Pericles, for instance, said that the vanishing
from their country of the young men who had fallen in the war
was 'as if the spring were taken out of the year'. Leptines, speaking
5　of the Lacedaemonians, said that he would not have the Athenians
let Greece 'lose one of her two eyes'. When Chares was pressing
for leave to be examined upon his share in the Olynthiac war,
Cephisodotus was indignant, saying that he wanted his examination to take place 'while he had his fingers upon the people's
throat'. The same speaker once urged the Athenians to march to
10　Euboea, 'with Miltiades' decree as their rations'. Iphicrates, indignant at the truce made by the Athenians with Epidaurus and the
neighbouring sea-board, said that they had stripped themselves of
their travelling money for the journey of war. Peitholaus called the
state-galley 'the people's big stick', and Sestos 'the corn-bin of the
15　Peiraeus'. Pericles bade his countrymen remove Aegina, 'that eye-
sore of the Peiraeus.' And Moerocles said he was no more a rascal
than was a certain respectable citizen he named, 'whose rascality
was worth over thirty per cent. per annum to him, instead of a
mere ten like his own'. There is also the iambic line of
Anaxandrides about the way his daughters put off marrying—

20　　　　　　　My daughters' marriage-bonds are overdue.

Polyeuctus said of a paralytic man named Speusippus that he
could not keep quiet, 'though fortune had fastened him in the pil-

lory of disease'. Cephisodotus called warships 'painted millstones'. Diogenes the Dog called taverns 'the mess-rooms of Attica'. Aesion   25
said that the Athenians had 'emptied' their town into Sicily: this is a graphic metaphor. 'Till all Hellas shouted aloud' may be regarded as a metaphor, and a graphic one again. Cephisodotus bade the Athenians take care not to hold too many 'parades'. Isocrates used the same word of those who 'parade' at the national festivals.   30
Another example occurs in the Funeral Speech: 'It is fitting that Greece should cut off her hair beside the tomb of those who fell at Salamis, since her freedom and their valour are buried in the same grave.' Even if the speaker here had only said that it was right to weep when valour was being buried in their grave, it would have   35
been a metaphor, and a graphic one; but the coupling of 'their val-   1411ᵇ
our' and 'her freedom' presents a kind of antithesis as well. 'The course of my words', said Iphicrates, 'lies straight through the middle of Chares' deeds': this is a proportional metaphor, and the phrase 'straight through the middle' makes it graphic. The expression 'to call in one danger to rescue us from another' is a graphic   5
metaphor. Lycoleon said, defending Chabrias, 'They did not respect even that bronze statue of his that intercedes for him yonder'. This was a metaphor for the moment, though it would not always apply; a vivid metaphor, however; Chabrias is in danger, and his statue intercedes for him—that lifeless yet living thing which records his services to his country. 'Practising in every way littleness   10
of mind' is metaphorical, for practising a quality implies increasing it. So is 'God kindled our reason to be a lamp within our souls', for both reason and light reveal things. So is 'we are not putting an end to our wars, but only postponing them', for both literal postpone-   15
ment and the making of such a peace as this apply to future action. So is such a saying as 'This treaty is a far nobler trophy than those we set up on fields of battle; *they* celebrate small gains and single successes; *it* celebrates our triumph in the war as a whole'; for both trophy and treaty are signs of victory. So is 'A country pays a heavy reckoning in being condemned by the judgement of mankind', for   20
a reckoning is damage deservedly incurred.

Chapter 11

It has already been mentioned that liveliness is got by using the proportional type of metaphor and by being graphic (ie. making your hearers *see* things). We have still to explain what we mean by their 'seeing things', and what must be done to effect this. By

25   'making them see things' I mean using expressions that represent
      things as in a state of activity. Thus, to say that a good man is 'four-
      square' is certainly a metaphor; both the good man and the square
      are perfect; but the metaphor does not suggest activity. On the
      other hand, in the expression 'with his vigour in full bloom' there
      is a notion of activity; and so in 'But you must roam as free as a sa-
      cred victim'; and in

30   Thereat up sprang the Hellenes to their feet,

      where 'up sprang' gives us activity as well as metaphor, for it at
      once suggests swiftness. So with Homer's common practice of giv-
      ing metaphorical life to lifeless things: all such passages are dis-
      tinguished by the effect of activity they convey. Thus,

          Downward anon to the valley rebounded the boulder *remorseless*;

      and

                          The (bitter) arrow *flew*;

      and

35   Flying on *eagerly*;

      and

1412ª   Stuck in the earth, still *panting* to feed on the flesh of the heroes;

      and

      And the point of the spear *in its fury* drove full through his breastbone.

      In all these examples the things have the effect of being active be-
      cause they are made into living beings; shameless behaviour and
      fury and so on are all forms of activity. And the poet has attached
5   these ideas to the things by means of proportional metaphors: as
      the stone is to Sisyphus, so is the shameless man to his victim. In
      his famous similes, too, he treats inanimate things in the same
      way:

      Curving and crested with white, host following host without ceasing.

      Here he represents everything as moving and living; and activity is
      movement.
          Metaphors must be drawn, as has been said already, from things
10   that are related to the original thing, and yet not obviously so
      related—just as in philosophy also an acute mind will perceive re-
      semblances even in things far apart. Thus Archytas said that an ar-
      bitrator and an altar were the same, since the injured fly to both

for refuge. Or you might say that an anchor and an overhead hook
were the same, since both are in a way the same, only the one secures things from below and the other from above. And to speak   15
of states as 'levelled' is to identify two widely different things, the
equality of a physical surface and the equality of political powers.

Liveliness is specially conveyed by metaphor, and by the further
power of surprising the hearer; because the hearer expected something different, his acquisition of the new idea impresses him all   20
the more. His mind seems to say, 'Yes, to be sure; I never thought
of that'. The liveliness of epigrammatic remarks is due to the
meaning not being just what the words say: as in the saying of
Stesichorus that 'the cicalas will chirp to themselves on the
ground'. Well-constructed riddles are attractive for the same reason; a new idea is conveyed, and there is metaphorical expression.
So with the 'novelties' of Theodorus. In these the thought is star-   25
tling, and, as Theodorus puts it, does not fit in with the ideas you
already have. They are like the burlesque words that one finds in
the comic writers. The effect is produced even by jokes depending
upon changes of the letters of a word; this too is a surprise. You
find this in verse as well as in prose. The word which comes is not
what the hearer imagined: thus

Onward he came, and his feet were shod with his—chilblains,   30

where one imagined the word would be 'sandals'. But the point
should be clear the moment the words are uttered. Jokes made by
altering the letters of a word consist in meaning, not just what you
say, but something that gives a twist to the word used; e.g. the remark of Theodorus about Nicon the harpist Θρᾷττ' εἶ σύ ('you
Thracian slavey'), where he pretends to mean θράττεις σύ ('you   35
harp-player'), and surprises us when we find he means something
else. So you enjoy the point when you see it, though the remark   1412b
will fall flat unless you are aware that Nicon is Thracian. Or again:
Βούλει αὐτὸν πέρσαι. In both these cases the saying must fit the
facts. This is also true of such lively remarks as the one to the effect that to the Athenians their empire (ἀρχή) of the sea was not
the beginning (ἀρχή) of their troubles, since they gained by it. Or   5
the opposite one of Isocrates, that their empire (ἀρχή) was the beginning (ἀρχή) of their troubles. Either way, the speaker says
something unexpected, the soundness of which is thereupon recognized. There would be nothing clever in saying 'empire is empire'. Isocrates means more than that, and uses the word with a
new meaning. So too with the former saying, which denies that
ἀρχή in one sense was ἀρχή in another sense. In all these jokes,   10

whether a word is used in a second sense or metaphorically, the joke is good if it fits the facts. For instance, Ἀνάσχετος (proper name) οὐκ ἀνασχετός: where you say that what is so-and-so in one sense is not so-and-so in another; well, if the man is unpleasant, the joke fits the facts. Again, take—

> Thou must not be a stranger stranger than
> Thou should'st.

15 Do not the words 'thou must not be', &c., amount to saying that the stranger must not always be strange? Here again is the use of one word in different senses. Of the same kind also is the much-praised verse of Anaxandrides:

> Death is most fit before you do
> Deeds that would make death fit for you.

This amounts to saying 'it is a fit thing to die when you are not fit to die', or 'it is a fit thing to die when death is not fit for you', i.e. 20 when death is not the fit return for what you are doing. The type of language employed is the same in all these examples; but the more briefly and antithetically such sayings can be expressed, the more taking they are, for antithesis impresses the new idea more firmly and brevity more quickly. They should always have either some personal application or some merit of expression, if they are 25 to be true without being common-place—two requirements not always satisfied simultaneously. Thus 'a man should die having done no wrong' is true but dull: 'the right man should marry the right woman' is also true but dull. No, there must be both good qualities together, as in 'it is fitting to die when you are not fit for death'. The more a saying has these qualities, the livelier it ap-30 pears: if, for instance, its wording is metaphorical, metaphorical in the right way, antithetical, and balanced, and at the same time it gives an idea of activity.

Successful similes also, as has been said above, are in a sense metaphors, since they always involve two relations like the pro-35 portional metaphor. Thus: a shield, we say, is the 'drinking-bowl 1413ᵃ of Ares', and a bow is the 'chordless lyre'. This way of putting a metaphor is not 'simple', as it would be if we called the bow a lyre or the shield a drinking-bowl. There are 'simple' similes also: we may say that a flute-player is like a monkey, or that a short-sighted man's eyes are like a lamp-flame with water dropping on it, since both eyes and flame keep winking. A simile succeeds best when it 5 is a converted metaphor, for it is possible to say that a shield *is like* the drinking-bowl of Ares, or that a ruin *is like* a house in rags, and

to say that Niceratus *is like* a Philoctetes stung by Pratys—the simile made by Thrasymachus when he saw Niceratus, who had been
beaten by Pratys in a recitation competition, still going about un-
kempt and unwashed. It is in these respects that poets fail worst   10
when they fail, and succeed best when they succeed, i.e. when
they give the resemblance pat, as in

> Those legs of his curl just like parsley leaves;

and

> Just like Philammon struggling with his punch-ball.

These are all similes; and that similes are metaphors has been
stated often already.

Proverbs, again, are metaphors from one species to another.
Suppose, for instance, a man to start some undertaking in hope of   15
gain and then to lose by it later on, 'Here we have once more the
man of Carpathus and his hare', says he. For both alike went
through the said experience.

It has now been explained fairly completely how liveliness is secured and why it has the effect it has. Successful hyperboles are
also metaphors, e.g. the one about the man with a black eye, 'you
would have thought he was a basket of mulberries'; here the 'black   20
eye' is compared to a mulberry because of its colour, the exaggeration lying in the quantity of mulberries suggested. The phrase
'*like* so-and-so' may introduce a hyperbole under the form of a
simile. Thus

> *Just like* Philammon struggling with his punch-ball

is equivalent to '*you would have thought he was* Philammon strug-   25
gling with his punch-ball'; and

> Those legs of his curl *just like* parsley leaves

is equivalent to 'his legs are so curly that *you would have thought*
they were not legs but parsley leaves'. Hyperboles are for young
men to use; they show vehemence of character; and this is why
angry people use them more than other people.   30

> Not though he gave me as much as the dust or the sands of the sea . . .
> But her, the daughter of Atreus' son, I never will marry,
> Nay, not though she were fairer than Aphrodite the Golden,
> Defter of hand than Athene . . .

(The Attic orators are particularly fond of this method of speech.)   1413ᵇ
Consequently it does not suit an elderly speaker.

Chapter 12

It should be observed that each kind of rhetoric has its own appropriate style. The style of written prose is not that of spoken oratory, nor are those of political and forensic speaking the same.
5 Both written and spoken have to be known. To know the latter is to know how to speak good Greek. To know the former means that you are not obliged, as otherwise you are, to hold your tongue when you wish to communicate something to the general public.

The written style is the more finished: the spoken better admits
10 of dramatic delivery—alike the kind of oratory that reflects character and the kind that reflects emotion. Hence actors look out for plays written in the latter style, and poets for actors competent to act in such plays. Yet poets whose plays are meant to be read *are* read and circulated: Chaeremon, for instance, who is as finished as a professional speech-writer; and Licymnius among the dithy-
15 rambic poets. Compared with those of others, the speeches of professional writers sound thin in actual contests. Those of the orators, on the other hand, are good to hear spoken, but look amateurish enough when they pass into the hands of a reader. This is just because they are so well suited for an actual tussle, and therefore contain many dramatic touches, which, being robbed of all dramatic rendering, fail to do their own proper work, and consequently look silly. Thus strings of unconnected words, and constant repetitions of words and phrases, are very properly con-
20 demned in written speeches: but not in spoken speeches—speakers use them freely, for they have a dramatic effect. In this repetition there must be variety of tone, paving the way, as it were, to dramatic effect; e.g. 'This is the villain among you who deceived you, who cheated you, who meant to betray you completely'. This is the sort of thing that Philemon the actor used to
25 do in the *Old Men's Madness* of Anaxandrides, whenever he spoke the words 'Rhadamanthus and Palamedes', and also in the prologue to the *Saints* whenever he pronounced the pronoun 'I'. If one does not deliver such things cleverly, it becomes a case of 'the man who swallowed a poker'. So too with strings of unconnected words, e.g. 'I came to him; I met him; I besought him'. Such pas-
30 sages must be *acted*, not delivered with the same quality and pitch of voice, as though they had only one idea in them. They have the further peculiarity of suggesting that a number of separate statements have been made in the time usually occupied by one. Just as the use of conjunctions makes many statements into a single one, so the omission of conjunctions acts in the reverse way and

makes a single one into many. It thus makes everything more important: e.g. 'I came to him; I talked to him; I entreated him' — what a lot of facts! the hearer thinks — 'he paid no attention to any- 1414ᵃ thing I said'. This is the effect which Homer seeks when he writes,

> Nireus likewise from Syme (three well-fashioned ships did bring),
> Nireus, the son of Aglaia (and Charopus, bright-faced king),
> Nireus, the comeliest man (of all that to Ilium's strand).

If many things are said about a man, his name must be mentioned many times; and therefore people think that, if his name is mentioned many times, many things have been said about him. So that Homer, by means of this illusion, has made a great deal of 5 Nireus though he has mentioned him only in this one passage, and has preserved his memory, though he nowhere says a word about him afterwards.

Now the style of oratory addressed to public assemblies is really just like scene-painting. The bigger the throng, the more distant is the point of view: so that, in the one and the other, high finish in detail is superfluous and seems better away. The forensic style is 10 more highly finished; still more so is the style of language addressed to a single judge, with whom there is very little room for rhetorical artifices, since he can take the whole thing in better, and judge of what is to the point and what is not; the struggle is less intense and so the judgement is undisturbed. This is why the same speakers do not distinguish themselves in all these branches at once; high finish is wanted least where dramatic delivery is 15 wanted most, and here the speaker must have a good voice, and above all, a strong one. It is ceremonial oratory that is most literary, for it is meant to be read; and next to it forensic oratory.

To analyse style still further, and add that it must be agreeable or magnificent, is useless; for why should it have these traits any more than 'restraint', 'liberality', or any other moral excellence? 20 Obviously agreeableness will be produced by the qualities already mentioned, if our definition of excellence of style has been correct. For what other reason should style be 'clear', and 'not mean' but 'appropriate'? If it is prolix, it is not clear; nor yet if it is curt. Plainly the middle way suits best. Again, style will be made agree- 25 able by the elements mentioned, namely by a good blending of ordinary and unusual words, by the rhythm, and by the persuasiveness that springs from appropriateness.

This concludes our discussion of style, both in its general aspects and in its special applications to the various branches of rhetoric. We have now to deal with Arrangement.

Chapter 13

30   A speech has two parts. You must state your case, and you must
prove it. You cannot either state your case and omit to prove it, or
prove it without having first stated it; since any proof must be a
proof of something, and the only use of a preliminary statement is
the proof that follows it. Of these two parts the first part is called
the Statement of the case, the second part the Argument, just as
35   we distinguish between Enunciation and Demonstration. The
current division is absurd. For 'narration' surely is part of a forensic speech only: how in a political speech or a speech of display
1414ᵇ can there be 'narration' in the technical sense? or a reply to a
forensic opponent? or an epilogue in closely-reasoned speeches?
Again, introduction, comparison of conflicting arguments, and recapitulation are only found in political speeches when there is a
struggle between two policies. They *may* occur then; so may even
accusation and defence, often enough; but they form no essential
5   part of a political speech. Even forensic speeches do not always
need epilogues; not, for instance, a short speech, nor one in which
the facts are easy to remember, the effect of an epilogue being always a reduction in the apparent length. It follows, then, that the
only necessary parts of a speech are the Statement and the
Argument. These are the essential features of a speech; and it cannot in any case have more than Introduction, Statement,
Argument, and Epilogue. 'Refutation of the Opponent' is part of
the arguments: so is 'Comparison' of the opponent's case with
10   your own, for that process is a magnifying of your own case and
therefore a part of the arguments, since one who does this *proves*
something. The Introduction does nothing like this; nor does the
Epilogue—it merely reminds us of what has been said already. If
we make such distinctions we shall end, like Theodorus and his
followers, by distinguishing 'narration' proper from 'post-
narration' and 'pre-narration', and 'refutation' from 'final refuta-
15   tion'. But we ought only to bring in a new name if it indicates a
real species with distinct specific qualities; otherwise the practice
is pointless and silly, like the way Licymnius invented names in
his *Art of Rhetoric*—'Secundation', 'Divagation', 'Ramification'.

Chapter 14

The Introduction is the beginning of a speech, corresponding to
20   the prologue in poetry and the prelude in flute-music; they are all

beginnings, paving the way, as it were, for what is to follow. The musical prelude resembles the introduction to speeches of display; as flute-players play first some brilliant passage they know well and then fit it on to the opening notes of the piece itself, so in speeches of display the writer should proceed in the same way; he should begin with what best takes his fancy, and then strike up his theme   25 and lead into it; which is indeed what *is* always done. (Take as an example the introduction to the *Helen* of Isocrates — there is nothing in common between the 'eristics' and Helen.) And here, even if you travel far from your subject, it is fitting, rather than that there should be sameness in the entire speech.

The usual subject for the introductions to speeches of display is   30 some piece of praise or censure. Thus Gorgias writes in his *Olympic Speech,* 'You deserve widespread admiration, men of Greece', praising thus those who started the festival gatherings. Isocrates, on the other hand, censures them for awarding distinctions to fine athletes but giving no prize for intellectual ability. Or one may begin with a piece of advice, thus: 'We ought to honour   35 good men and so I myself am praising Aristeides' or 'We ought to honour those who are unpopular but not bad men, men whose good qualities have never been noticed, like Alexander son of Priam.' Here the orator gives *advice.* Or we may begin as speakers   1415ª do in the law-courts; that is to say, with appeals to the audience to excuse us if our speech is about something paradoxical, difficult, or hackneyed; like Choerilus in the lines —

> But now when allotment of all has been made . . .

Introductions to speeches of display, then, may be composed of   5 some piece of praise or censure, of advice to do or not to do something, or of appeals to the audience; and you must choose between making these preliminary passages connected or disconnected with the speech itself.

Introductions to forensic speeches, it must be observed, have the same value as the prologues of dramas and the introductions to epic poems; the dithyrambic prelude resembling the introduction to a speech of display, as   10

> For thee, and thy gifts, and thy battle-spoils . . .

In prologues, and in epic poetry, a foretaste of the theme is given, intended to inform the hearers of it in advance instead of keeping their minds in suspense. Anything vague puzzles them: so give them a grasp of the beginning, and they can hold fast to it and follow the argument. So we find —   15

Sing, O goddess of song, of the Wrath . . .

Tell me, O Muse, of the hero . . .

Lead me to tell a new tale, how there came great warfare to Europe
Out of the Asian land . . .

The tragic poets, too, let us know the pivot of their play; if not
at the outset like Euripides, at least somewhere in the preface to a
20 speech like Sophocles—

Polybus was my father . . . ;

and so in Comedy. This, then, is the most essential function and
distinctive property of the introduction, to show what the aim of
the speech is; and therefore no introduction ought to be employed
where the subject is not long or intricate.

25 The other kinds of introduction employed are remedial in purpose, and may be used in any type of speech. They are concerned
with the speaker, the hearer, the subject, or the speaker's opponent. Those concerned with the speaker himself or with his opponent are directed to removing or exciting prejudice. But
whereas the defendant will begin by dealing with this sort of thing,
the prosecutor will take quite another line and deal with such
30 matters in the closing part of his speech. The reason for this is not
far to seek. The defendant, when he is going to bring himself on
the stage, must clear away any obstacles, and therefore must begin
by removing any prejudice felt against him. But if you are to *excite*
prejudice, you must do so at the close, so that the judges may
more easily remember what you have said.

The appeal to the hearer aims at securing his goodwill, or at
35 arousing his resentment, or sometimes at gaining his serious attention to the case, or even at distracting it—for gaining it is not
always an advantage, and speakers will often for that reason try to
make him laugh.

You may use any means you choose to make your hearer re-
ceptive; among others, giving him a good impression of your character, which always helps to secure his attention. He will be ready
1415ᵇ to attend to anything that touches himself, and to anything that is
important, surprising, or agreeable; and you should accordingly
convey to him the impression that what you have to say is of this
nature. If you wish to distract his attention, you should imply that
the subject does not affect him, or is trivial or disagreeable. But
5 observe, all this has nothing to do with the speech itself. It merely
has to do with the weak-minded tendency of the hearer to listen to
what is beside the point. Where this tendency is absent, no intro-

duction is wanted beyond a summary statement of your subject, to
put a sort of head on the main body of your speech. Moreover,
calls for attention, when required, may come equally well in any
part of a speech; in fact, the beginning of it is just where there is
least slackness of interest; it is therefore ridiculous to put this kind
of thing at the beginning, when every one is listening with most attention. Choose therefore any point in the speech where such an
appeal is needed, and then say 'Now I beg you to note this point—
it concerns you quite as much as myself'; or

> I will tell you that whose like you have never yet

heard for terror, or for wonder. This is what Prodicus called 'slip-
ping in a bit of the fifty-drachma show-lecture for the audience
whenever they began to nod'. It is plain that such introductions
are addressed not to ideal hearers, but to hearers as we find them.
The use of introductions to excite prejudice or to dispel misgivings
is universal—

> My lord, I will not say that eagerly . . .

or

> Why all this preface?

Introductions are popular with those whose case is weak, or looks
weak; it pays them to dwell on anything rather than the actual
facts of it. That is why slaves, instead of answering the questions
put to them, make indirect replies with long preambles. The
means of exciting in your hearers goodwill and various other feelings of the same kind have already been described. The poet
finely says

May I find in Phaeacian hearts, at my coming, goodwill and compassion;

and these are the two things we should aim at. In speeches of display we must make the hearer feel that the eulogy includes either
himself or his family or his way of life or something or other of the
kind. For it is true, as Socrates says in the *Funeral Speech,* that 'the
difficulty is not to praise the Athenians at Athens but at Sparta'.

The introductions of political oratory will be made out of the
same materials as those of the forensic kind, though the nature of
political oratory makes them very rare. The subject is known already, and therefore the *facts* of the case need no introduction; but
you may have to say something on account of yourself or your opponents; or those present may be inclined to treat the matter
either more or less seriously than you wish them to. You may

accordingly have to excite or dispel some prejudice, or to make the
matter under discussion seem more or less important than before:
for either of which purposes you will want an introduction. You
may also want one to add elegance to your remarks, feeling that
1416ᵃ otherwise they will have a casual air, like Gorgias' eulogy of the
Eleans, in which, without any preliminary sparring or fencing, he
begins straight off with 'Happy city of Elis!'

Chapter 15

In dealing with prejudice, one class of argument is that whereby
you can dispel objectionable suppositions about yourself. It makes
5   no practical difference whether such a supposition has been put
into words or not, so that this distinction may be ignored. Another
way is to meet any of the issues directly: to deny the alleged fact;
or to say that you have done no harm, or none to *him*, or not as
much as he says; or that you have done him no injustice, or not
much; or that you have done nothing disgraceful, or nothing disgraceful enough to matter: these are the sort of questions on which
the dispute hinges. Thus Iphicrates, replying to Nausicrates, ad-
10 mitted that he had done the deed alleged, and that he had done
Nausicrates harm, but not that he had done him wrong. Or you
may admit the wrong, but balance it with other facts, and say that,
if the deed harmed him, at any rate it was honourable; or that, if
it gave him pain, at least it did him good; or something else like
that. Another way is to allege that your action was due to mistake,
15 or bad luck, or necessity—as Sophocles said he was not trembling,
as his traducer maintained, in order to make people think him an
old man, but because he could not help it; he would rather *not* be
eighty years old. You may balance your motive against your actual
deed; saying, for instance, that you did not mean to injure him but
to do so-and-so; that you did not do what you are falsely charged
with doing—the damage was accidental—'I should indeed be a
20 detestable person if I had deliberately intended this result.'
Another way is open when your calumniator, or any of his connexions, is or has been subject to the same grounds for suspicion.
Yet another, when others are subject to the same grounds for suspicion but are admitted to be in fact innocent of the charge: e.g.
'Must I be a profligate because I am well-groomed? Then so-and-
so must be one too.' Another, if other people have been calumni-
25 ated by the same man or some one else, or, without being calumniated, have been suspected, like yourself now, and yet have been

proved innocent. Another way is to return calumny for calumny and say, 'It is monstrous to trust the man's statements when you cannot trust the man himself.' Another is when the question has been already decided. So with Euripides' reply to Hygiaenon, who, in the action for an exchange of properties, accused him of impiety in having written a line encouraging perjury— 30

> My tongue hath sworn: no oath is on my soul.

Euripides said that his opponent himself was guilty in bringing into the law-courts cases whose decision belonged to the Dionysiac contests. 'If I have not already answered for my words there, I am ready to do so if you choose to prosecute me there.' Another method is to denounce calumny, showing what an enormity it is, and in particular that it raises false issues, and that it 35 means a lack of confidence in the merits of his case. The argument from evidential circumstances is available for both parties: thus in the *Teucer* Odysseus says that Teucer is closely bound to 1416ᵇ Priam, since his mother Hesione was Priam's sister. Teucer replies that Telamon his father was Priam's enemy, and that he himself did not betray the spies to Priam. Another method, suitable for the calumniator, is to praise some trifling merit at great length, and then attack some important failing concisely; or after mentioning 5 a number of good qualities to attack one bad one that really bears on the question. This is the method of thoroughly skilful and unscrupulous prosecutors. By mixing up the man's merits with what is bad, they do their best to make use of them to damage him.

There is another method open to both calumniator and apologist. Since a given action can be done from many motives, the former must try to disparage it by selecting the worse motive of two, 10 the latter to put the better construction on it. Thus one might argue that Diomedes chose Odysseus as his companion because he supposed Odysseus to be the best man for the purpose; and you might reply to this that it was, on the contrary, because he was the only hero so worthless that Diomedes need not fear his rivalry.

Chapter 16

We may now pass from the subject of calumny to that of Narration. 15

Narration in ceremonial oratory is not continuous but intermittent. There must, of course, be some survey of the actions that form the subject-matter of the speech. The speech is a composi-

tion containing two parts. One of these is not provided by the orator's art, viz. the actions themselves, of which the orator is in no
20 sense author. The other part is provided by his art, namely, the
proof (where proof is needed) that the actions were done, the description of their quality or of their extent, or even all these three
things together. Now the reason why sometimes it is not desirable
to make the whole narrative continuous is that the case thus ex-
pounded is hard to keep in mind. Show, therefore, from one set of
facts that your hero is, e.g. brave, and from other sets of facts that
he is able, just, &c. A speech thus arranged is comparatively sim-
25 ple, instead of being complicated and elaborate. You will have to
recall well-known deeds among others; and because they are well-
known, the hearer usually needs no narration of them; none, for
instance, if your object is the praise of Achilles; we all know the
facts of his life—what you have to do is to apply those facts. But if
your object is the praise of Critias, you *must* narrate his deeds,
which not many people know of . . .

Nowadays it is said, absurdly enough, that the narration should
30 be rapid. Remember what the man said to the baker who asked
whether he was to make the cake hard or soft: 'What, can't you
make it *right*?' Just so here. We are not to make long narrations,
just as we are not to make long introductions or long arguments.
35 Here, again, rightness does not consist either in rapidity or in conciseness, but in the happy mean; that is, in saying just so much as
will make the facts plain, or will lead the hearer to believe that the
1417ᵃ thing has happened, or that the man has caused injury or wrong
to some one, or that the facts are really as important as you wish
them to be thought: or the opposite facts to establish the opposite
arguments.

You may also narrate as you go anything that does credit to yourself, e.g. 'I kept telling him to do his duty and not abandon his
children'; or discredit to your adversary, e.g. 'But he answered me
5 that, wherever he might find himself, there he would find other
children', the answer Herodotus records of the Egyptian muti-
neers. Slip in anything else that the judges will enjoy.

The defendant will make less of the narration. He has to maintain that the thing has not happened, or did no harm, or was not
unjust, or not so bad as is alleged. He must therefore not waste
10 time about what is admitted fact, unless this bears on his own contention; e.g. that the thing was done, but was not wrong. Further,
we must speak of events as past and gone, except where they excite
pity or indignation by being represented as present. The Story told
to Alcinous is an example of a brief chronicle, when it is repeated

to Penelope in sixty lines. Another instance is the Epic Cycle as
treated by Phayllus, and the prologue to the *Oeneus*.   15

The narration should depict character; to which end you must
know what makes it do so. One such thing is the indication of
moral purpose; the quality of purpose indicated determines the
quality of character depicted and is itself determined by the end
pursued. Thus it is that mathematical discourses depict no character; they have nothing to do with moral purpose, for they represent nobody as pursuing any end. On the other hand, the Socratic
dialogues do depict character, being concerned with moral ques-   20
tions. This end will also be gained by describing the manifestations of various types of character, e.g. 'he kept walking along as
he talked', which shows the man's recklessness and rough man-
ners. Do not let your words seem inspired so much by intelligence, in the manner now current, as by moral purpose: e.g. 'I
willed this; aye, it was my moral purpose; true, I gained nothing   25
by it, still it is better thus.' For the other way shows good sense, but
this shows good character; good sense making us go after what is
useful, and good character after what is noble. Where any detail
may appear incredible, then add the cause of it; of this Sophocles
provides an example in the *Antigone*, where Antigone says she had
cared more for her brother than for husband or children, since if
the latter perished they might be replaced,   30

> But since my father and mother in their graves
> Lie dead, no brother can be born to me.

If you have no such cause to suggest, just say that you are aware
that no one will believe your words, but the fact remains that such
is your nature, however hard the world may find it to believe that   35
a man deliberately does anything except what pays him.

Again, you must make use of the emotions. Relate the familiar
manifestations of them, and those that distinguish yourself and
your opponent; for instance, 'he went away scowling at me'. So
Aeschines described Cratylus as 'hissing with fury and shaking his   1417ᵇ
fists'. These details carry conviction: the audience take the truth
of what they know as so much evidence for the truth of what they
do not. Plenty of such details may be found in Homer:

> Thus did she say: but the old woman buried her face in her hands: 5

a true touch—people beginning to cry do put their hands over
their eyes.

Bring yourself on the stage from the first in the right character,
that people may regard you in that light; and the same with your

adversary; but do not let them see what you are about. How easily
such impressions may be conveyed we can see from the way in
10   which we get some inkling of things we know nothing of by the
mere look of the messenger bringing news of them. Have some
narrative in many different parts of your speech; and sometimes
let there be none at the beginning of it.

In political oratory there is very little opening for narration; nobody can 'narrate' what has not yet happened. If there is narration
at all, it will be of past events, the recollection of which is to help
15   the hearers to make better plans for the future. Or it may be employed to attack some one's character, or to eulogize him—only
then you will not be doing what the political speaker, as such, has
to do.

If any statement you make is hard to believe, you must guaran-
tee its truth, and at once offer an explanation, and then furnish it
with such particulars as will be expected. Thus Carcinus' Jocasta,
in his *Oedipus*, keeps guaranteeing the truth of her answers to the
20   inquiries of the man who is seeking her son; and so with Haemon
in Sophocles.   .

Chapter 17

The duty of the Arguments is to attempt demonstrative proofs.
These proofs must bear directly upon the question in dispute,
which must fall under one of four heads. (1) If you maintain that
25   the act *was not committed*, your main task in court is to prove this.
(2) If you maintain that the act *did no harm*, prove this. If you
maintain that (3) the act was *less* than is alleged, or (4) *justified*,
prove these facts, just as you would prove the act not to have been
committed if you were maintaining that.

It should be noted that only where the question in dispute falls
under the first of these heads can it be true that one of the two parties is necessarily a rogue. Here ignorance cannot be pleaded, as
it might if the dispute were whether the act was justified or not.
30   This argument must therefore be used in this case only, not in the
others.

In ceremonial speeches you will develop your case mainly by
arguing that what has been done is, e.g., noble and useful. The
facts themselves are to be taken on trust; proof of them is only sub-
mitted on those rare occasions when they are not easily credible or
when they have been set down to some one else.
35   In political speeches you may maintain that a proposal is im-

practicable; or that, though practicable, it is unjust, or will do no good, or is not so important as its proposer thinks. Note any false-hoods about irrelevant matters—they will look like proof that his other statements also are false. Argument by 'example' is highly 1418ᵃ suitable for political oratory, argument by 'enthymeme' better suits forensic. Political oratory deals with future events, of which it can do no more than quote past events as examples. Forensic ora-tory deals with what is or is not *now* true, which can better be demonstrated, because not contingent—there is no contingency in what has now already happened. Do not use a continuous suc-cession of enthymemes: intersperse them with other matter, or   5 they will spoil one another's effect. There are limits to their number—

Friend, you have spoken *as much* as a sensible man would have spoken.—

'as *much*' says Homer, not 'as *well*'. Nor should you try to make en-thymemes on every point; if you do, you will be acting just like some students of philosophy, whose conclusions are more familiar   10 and believable than the premises from which they draw them. And avoid the enthymeme form when you are trying to rouse feel-ing; for it will either kill the feeling or will itself fall flat: all simul-taneous motions tend to cancel each other either completely or partially. Nor should you go after the enthymeme form in a pas-sage where you are depicting character—the process of demon-   15 stration can express neither moral character nor moral purpose. Maxims should be employed in the Arguments—and in the Narration too—since these do express character: 'I have given him this, though I am quite aware that one should "Trust no man".' Or if you are appealing to the emotions: 'I do not regret it, though I have been wronged; if he has the profit on his side, I have justice   20 on mine.'

Political oratory is a more difficult task than forensic; and natu-rally so, since it deals with the future, whereas the pleader deals with the past, which, as Epimenides of Crete said, even the divin-ers already know. (Epimenides did not practise divination about the future; only about the obscurities of the past.) Besides, in   25 forensic oratory you have a basis in the law; and once you have a starting-point, you can prove anything with comparative ease. Then again, political oratory affords few chances for those leisurely digressions in which you may attack your adversary, talk about yourself, or work on your hearers' emotions; fewer chances, indeed, than any other affords, unless your set purpose is to divert

your hearers' attention. Accordingly, if you find yourself in diffi-
30 culties, follow the lead of the Athenian speakers, and that of
Isocrates, who makes regular attacks upon people in the course of
a political speech, e.g. upon the Lacedaemonians in the
Panegyricus, and upon Chares in the speech about the allies. In
ceremonial oratory, intersperse your speech with bits of episodic
eulogy, like Isocrates, who is always bringing some one forward for
this purpose. And this is what Gorgias meant by saying that he al-
35 ways found something to talk about. For if he speaks of Achilles,
he praises Peleus, then Aeacus, then Zeus; and in like manner the
virtue of valour, describing its good results, and saying what it
is like.

Now if you have proofs to bring forward, bring them forward,
and your moral discourse as well; if you have no enthymemes,
1418ᵇ then fall back upon moral discourse: after all, it is more fitting for
a good man to display himself as an honest fellow than as a subtle
reasoner. Refutative enthymemes are more popular than demonstrative ones: their logical cogency is more striking: the facts about
two opposites always stand out clearly when the two are put side
by side.

5   The 'Reply to the Opponent' is not a separate division of the
speech; it is part of the Arguments to break down the opponent's
case, whether by objection or by counter-syllogism. Both in political speaking and when pleading in court, if you are the first
speaker you should put your own arguments forward first, and
then meet the arguments on the other side by refuting them and
pulling them to pieces beforehand. If, however, the case for the
other side contains a great variety of arguments, begin with these,
10 like Callistratus in the Messenian assembly, when he demolished
the arguments likely to be used against him before giving his own.
If you speak later, you must first, by means of refutation and
counter-syllogism, attempt some answer to your opponent's
speech, especially if his arguments have been well received. For
just as our minds refuse a favourable reception to a *person* against
15 whom they are prejudiced, so they refuse it to a speech when they
have been favourably impressed by the speech on the other side.
You should, therefore, make room in the minds of the audience
for your coming speech; and this will be done by getting your opponent's speech out of the way. So attack that first—either the
whole of it, or the most important, successful, or vulnerable
20 points in it, and thus inspire confidence in what you have to say
yourself—

> First, champion will I be of Goddesses . . .
> Never, I ween, would Hera . . . :

where the speaker has attacked the silliest argument first. So much
for the Arguments.

With regard to the element of moral character: there are asser-
tions which, if made about yourself, may excite dislike, appear te-
dious, or expose you to the risk of contradiction; and other things   25
which you cannot say about your opponent without seeming abusive or ill-bred. Put such remarks, therefore, into the mouth of
some third person. This is what Isocrates does in the *Philippus* and
in the *Antidosis*, and Archilochus in his satires. The latter represents the father himself as attacking his daughter in the lampoon

> Think nought impossible at all,
> Nor swear that it shall not befall . . .

and puts into the mouth of Charon the carpenter the lampoon   30
which begins

> Not for the wealth of Gyges. . . .

So too Sophocles makes Haemon appeal to his father on behalf of
Antigone as if it were others who were speaking.

Again, sometimes you should restate your enthymemes in the
form of maxims; e.g. 'Wise men will come to terms in the hour of
success; for they will gain most if they do'. Expressed as an en-   35
thymeme, this would run, 'If we ought to come to terms when
doing so will enable us to gain the greatest advantage, *then* we
ought to come to terms in the hour of success.'

Chapter 18

Next as to Interrogation. The best moment to employ this is when
your opponent has so answered one question that the putting of   1419ª
just one more lands him in absurdity. Thus Pericles questioned
Lampon about the way of celebrating the rites of the Saviour
Goddess. Lampon declared that no uninitiated person could be
told of them. Pericles then asked, 'Do you know them yourself?'
'Yes', answered Lampon. 'Why,' said Pericles, 'how can that be,
when you are uninitiated?'   5

Another good moment is when one premiss of an argument is
obviously true, and you can see that your opponent must say 'yes'
if you ask him whether the other is true. Having first got this

answer about the other, do not go on to ask him about the obviously true one, but just state the conclusion yourself. Thus, when
Meletus denied that Socrates believed in the existence of gods but
10 admitted that he talked about a supernatural power, Socrates pro-
ceeded to ask whether 'supernatural beings were not either children of the gods or in some way divine?' 'Yes', said Meletus.
'Then', replied Socrates, 'is there any one who believes in the existence of children of the gods and yet not in the existence of the
gods themselves?' Another good occasion is when you expect to
show that your opponent is contradicting either his own words or
what every one believes. A fourth is when it is impossible for him
to meet your question except by an evasive answer. If he answers
15 'True, and yet not true', or 'Partly true and partly not true', or 'True
in one sense but not in another', the audience thinks he is in dif-
ficulties, and applauds his discomfiture. In other cases do not attempt interrogation; for if your opponent gets in an objection, you
are felt to have been worsted. You cannot ask a series of questions
owing to the incapacity of the audience to follow them; and for
this reason you should also make your enthymemes as compact as
possible.

20   In replying, you must meet ambiguous questions by drawing
reasonable distinctions, not by a curt answer. In meeting questions
that seem to involve you in a contradiction, offer the explanation
at the outset of your answer, before your opponent asks the next
question or draws his conclusion. For it is not difficult to see the
drift of his argument in advance. This point, however, as well as
the various means of refutation, may be regarded as known to us
from the *Topics*.

25   When your opponent in drawing his conclusion puts it in the
form of a question, you must justify your answer. Thus when
Sophocles was asked by Peisander whether he had, like the other
members of the Board of Safety, voted for setting up the Four
Hundred, he said 'Yes.' 'Why, did you not think it wicked?'
— 'Yes.' — 'So *you* committed this wickedness?' — 'Yes', said
30 Sophocles, 'for there was nothing better to do.' Again, the
Lacedaemonian, when he was being examined on his conduct as
ephor, was asked whether he thought that the other ephors had
been justly put to death. 'Yes', he said. 'Well then', asked his opponent, 'did not *you* propose the same measures as they?' —
'Yes.' — 'Well then, would not *you* too be justly put to death?' —
35 'Not at all', said he; '*they* were bribed to do it, and I did it from
conviction'. Hence you should not ask any further questions after
1419ᵇ drawing the conclusion, nor put the conclusion itself in the form

of a further question, unless there is a large balance of truth on your side.

As to jests. These are supposed to be of some service in controversy. Gorgias said that you should kill your opponents' earnestness with jesting and their jesting with earnestness; in which he was right. Jests have been classified in the *Poetics*. Some are becoming to a gentleman, others are not; see that you choose such as become *you*. Irony better befits a gentleman than buffoonery; the ironical man jokes to amuse himself, the buffoon to amuse other people.

Chapter 19

The Epilogue has four parts. You must (1) make the audience   10
well-disposed towards yourself and ill-disposed towards your opponent, (2) magnify or minimize the leading facts, (3) excite the required state of emotion in your hearers, and (4) refresh their memories.

(1) Having shown your own truthfulness and the untruthfulness of your opponent, the natural thing is to commend yourself, censure him, and hammer in your points. You must aim at one of two   15
objects—you must make yourself out a good man and him a bad one either in yourselves or in relation to your hearers. How this is to be managed—by what lines of argument you are to represent people as good or bad—this has been already explained.

(2) The facts having been proved, the natural thing to do next   20
is to magnify or minimize their importance. The facts must be admitted before you can discuss how important they are; just as the body cannot grow except from something already present. The proper lines of argument to be used for this purpose of amplification and depreciation have already been set forth.

(3) Next, when the facts and their importance are clearly understood, you must excite your hearers' emotions. These emotions   25
are pity, indignation, anger, hatred, envy, emulation, pugnacity. The lines of argument to be used for these purposes also have been previously mentioned.

(4) Finally you have to review what you have already said. Here you may properly do what some wrongly recommend doing in the introduction—repeat your points frequently so as to make them   30
easily understood. What you *should* do in your introduction is to state your subject, in order that the point to be judged may be quite plain; in the epilogue you should summarize the arguments

by which your case has been proved. The first step in this review-
ing process is to observe that you have done what you undertook
to do. You must, then, state what you have said and why you have
said it. Your method may be a comparison of your own case with
35   that of your opponent; and you may compare either the ways you
have both handled the same point or make your comparison less
direct: 'My opponent said so-and-so on this point; I said so-and-so,
1420ᵃ and this is why I said it'. Or with modest irony, e.g. 'He certainly
said so-and-so, but I said so-and-so'. Or 'How vain he would have
been if he had proved all this instead of *that!*' Or put it in the form
of a question, 'What has *not* been proved by me?' or 'What *has* my
opponent proved?' You may proceed then, either in this way by
setting point against point, or by following the natural order of the
1420ᵇ arguments as spoken, first giving your own, and then separately, if
you wish, those of your opponent.

For the conclusion, the disconnected style of language is appropriate, and will mark the difference between the oration and
the peroration. 'I have done. You have heard me. The facts are before you. I ask for your judgement.'

INDEX

References are to the chapter and line numbers shown
in the outer margin of the text.

DOVER THRIFT EDITIONS

UNABRIDGED

Short Stories, Louisa May Alcott. (0-486-29063-8)

Winesburg, Ohio, Sherwood Anderson. (0-486-28269-4)

O Pioneers! Willa Cather. (0-486-27785-2)

The Awakening, Kate Chopin. (0-486-27786-0)

Selected Poems, Emily Dickinson. (0-486-26466-1)

Self-Reliance and Other Essays, Ralph Waldo Emerson. (0-486-27790-9)

This Side of Paradise, F. Scott Fitzgerald. (0-486-28999-0)

The Autobiography of Benjamin Franklin. (0-486-29073-5)

The Road Not Taken and Other Poems, Robert Frost. (Available in U.S. only.) (0-486-27550-7)

The Scarlet Letter, Nathaniel Hawthorne. (0-486-28048-9)

Washington Square, Henry James. (0-486-40431-5)

The Country of the Pointed Firs, Sarah Orne Jewett. (0-486-28196-5)

The Story of My Life, Helen Keller. (0-486-29249-5)

Great Speeches, Abraham Lincoln. (0-486-26872-1)

Evangeline and Other Poems, Henry Wadsworth Longfellow. (0-486-28255-4)

Spoon River Anthology, Edgar Lee Masters. (0-486-27275-3)

Renascence and Other Poems, Edna St. Vincent Millay. (Available in U.S. only.) (0-486-26873-X)

Civil War Poetry: An Anthology, Paul Negri, ed. (0-486-29883-3)

The Gold-Bug and Other Tales, Edgar Allan Poe. (0-486-26875-6)

Great Poems by American Women: An Anthology, Susan Rattiner, ed. (0-486-40164-2)

Native American Songs and Poems: An Anthology, Brian Swann, ed. (0-486-29450-1)

Adventures of Huckleberry Finn, Mark Twain. (0-486-28061-6)

Up from Slavery, Booker T. Washington. (0-486-28738-6)

Ethan Frome, Edith Wharton. (0-486-26690-7)

Selected Poems, Walt Whitman. (0-486-26878-0)